A Gathering of Memories

A Gathering of Memories

Family, Nation, and Church in a Forgetful World

CHARLES R. PINCHES

Brazos Press
Grand Rapids, Michigan

© 2006 by Charles R. Pinches

Published by Brazos Press
a division of Baker Publishing Group
P.O. Box 6287, Grand Rapids, MI 49516-6287
www.brazospress.com

Printed in the United States of America

Library of Congress Cataloging-in-Publication Data
Pinches, Charles Robert.
      A gathering of memories : family, nation, and church in a forgetful world /
   Charles R. Pinches.
          p.   cm.
      Includes bibliographical references.
      ISBN 1-58743-104-1 (pbk.)
          1. Memory—Religious aspects—Christianity. 2. Memory—Social aspects.
   I. Title.
   BV4597.565.P56 2006
   260—dc22   2005028471

For Robin
with admiration, gratitude, and love

Contents

Preface   9
Introduction: Memory Awakened   15

Part I Family
1. The Body in the Family: A Wanderer and His Old Nurse   29
2. Sadness in the Family: Learning from David's Regret   45
3. Redemption Comes to the Family   61

Part II Nation
4. Memory, Patriotism, and the Confession of Our Sins   77
5. National Memory at Gettysburg   93
6. In the Country of the Savior   107

Part III Church
7. In Moses's Memory   123
8. A Dinner to Remember . . . but Judas Leaves before Dessert   139
9. Re-membering by Baptism   157

Works Cited   171

Preface

This book began early in 2002 when I traveled to Texas to speak to the Texas Baptist's Christian Life Conference. Questions of memory had long been on my mind, but the topic was not much discussed in public. Suddenly, after September 11, 2001, talk of remembering was everywhere. In those days immediately following the terrorist attacks, Americans sensed a deep hunger for something, coupled with bewilderment about what to do about it. Chapter eight of this book was my initial attempt to draw out some suggestions for the Texas Baptists.

Only a few academics came to that conference; most in the audience were pastors or interested lay people—people whose challenge daily is to live out their Christian faith in workplace or family life in America. Could the church or its theologians say anything to them about memory that did not require a return to graduate study in theology? The talk I gave to the Texas Baptists was my first attempt to answer that question. Afterwards, response from my brother-in-law Scott Bolinder, who publishes books, and Brent Laytham at the Ekklesia Project, who enthusiastically distributed the talk in pamphlet form, encouraged me to stretch what I had said in Texas into a book. And so I began to write. My resolve was to avoid at every turn the heaviness by which theological writing can become weighed down, while at the same time engaging an important, broad, and comprehensive subject in a variety of ways. By its very nature, theology takes aim at the most vital and substantial things; it is too bad if it must become boring along the way.

This resolve to keep things in simple terms challenged me throughout. Memory is complicated. We use the word frequently, with a wide spray of meanings. Part of the task of this book is to sort this usage out. It helps to combine "memory" with "identity," as Pope John Paul II did

in the title of his last book before dying. The idea is that if we forget we
will lose our identity. For John Paul II, this is not just for individuals
suffering identity crises, but for whole peoples, primarily those in the
Western "developed" world. On his account, there is a battle raging for
the corporate human soul—and it is being played out in the fields of
memory and forgetfulness in places like Poland where Western ideas
of "cultural progress," all tied up with money and technology and unbounded individual freedom of choice, spar with the deeply spiritual
history of the Polish people, dating as far back as its "baptism" at the
beginning of the eleventh century.

As I shall suggest in what follows, memory and identity loss is an
especially pressing problem in the modern (or postmodern) Western
world, where the pope thinks it has reached crisis level. But perhaps
it is not only a modern problem, a point we can get from recollecting
the very ancient story of Odysseus. Another way to mark the age of the
problem of memory is to dig into the center of the Decalogue, right between the duties we owe to God and those we owe to our fellow human
beings, where we find this: "Honor your father and your mother, so that
your days may be long in the land that the LORD your God is giving you"
(Exod. 20:12).

Memory brings the past to us in many ways, but nowhere more directly and forcefully than through family. Moses knew this, and so did
Homer. This is where I want to start with memory. Yet this is not a book
all about family piety and values. Jesus, whom Christians claim to follow, was not exactly bursting at the seams with family piety. Consider
Luke's story, the only one in the Bible about Jesus's adolescence. Jesus
(age 12) stays late talking with scholars in the temple, and the family
leaves without him. When they are reunited, his mother Mary takes him
to task (Luke 2:48–50). But Jesus has roughly this to say in reply: "Look,
Mom, don't forget that this is not really all about you and Joseph having
an anxiety-free parental experience."

Christians will want to say that Jesus kept the commandment about
honoring his parents here, but his way of doing it surprised both them
and us. This is the thing to do with memory: start with family, and then
see what surprising new place Christians will need to go to next. I follow
this pattern in this book. We start with family and end with church. To
get the flow, though, we shall need to work over the ground of family
quite thoroughly, including the ground that connects it with nation. As I
hope to show, family is especially important for memory since it relates
so deeply to body (we get our bodies from our parents, of course) and,
as the commandment about honoring our parents marks, to land, which
is a kind of body itself, the one from which we receive bodily life and
sustenance. Family is memory's most natural home.

In the first chapters of this book I am depending on my readers to have a sense of the memory that is carried by families. I believe this is easy; we did not need Freud to tell us that the first place our faculty of memory takes us when we look back on our individual lives is to childhood and family. But, as this is not a book about family piety, it is also not a book about individual memories of childhood. No doubt we need some connection to a particular past remembered to engage the topic of memory. As the author of this book, on occasion I offer some of my own memories, most of them connected in some way or another with family. Yet as I try to point out in various ways, family memories, as well as national memories, can quickly turn sentimental, dangerously so, if they are not tested against other truths. For Christians this must be scripture. Scripture is, in one sense, all about memory. In it we are given a past. As we receive this gift we must see—perhaps as the young Jesus was schooling his mother—that it is not really all about us.

So, two things I try never to leave behind in the book: family memories (which are also bodily memories) and the biblical text. If it is true, as I allege, that memory in our time is slipping, and even partly true, as the pope alleged, that the battle for memory in the modern world is the battle for its soul, then we are going to need to look around for some help in reclamation and rehabilitation. I do not think we can do better than with these two sources.

While this is not an academic book, there are some academic matters bubbling in the background. For instance, I have called the family "natural." There is weight in this word, I know. In theological circles we have been frightened away from it, most recently by worries that the use of, for instance, "natural law" language in ethics will make us water down the Christian gospel. Given the history of Protestant liberalism, fundamentalism, and Catholic neo-scholastic thinking of the past two centuries, this worry has some grounding. My own teacher and good friend Stanley Hauerwas has carried this worry as a burden for us all, and he has done an extraordinary job of getting the word out about it.

In my more academic theological writings I have depended on Hauerwas for a great deal. The dependence continues in this book. Indeed, I had the good fortune to arrive at graduate school when Professor Hauerwas was writing essays whose explosive power in the discipline of Christian ethics, I think, has yet to be surpassed in his own work and that of his contemporaries. One of these was "Memory as a Moral Task." When I say that memory has been long on my mind, what I really mean is that that essay has never left me. Moreover, Hauerwas taught me, as another of his essays from this period marks, the significance of "keeping theological ethics imaginative"—something I hope this book also does.

That said, in this book I deviate from certain trajectories in Hauerwas's thought. My use of the word "natural" is a signal of this. In academic terms, I think that theologians like Jean Porter are wise to attempt to rehabilitate natural law thinking, not over against, but with the help of biblical and theological reflection. I also believe, with Porter, that any full-bodied return to the structure of Aquinas's thought will require this rehabilitation.

My deviation from Hauerwas shows up, I think, in the relations I try to accent as I turn a corner in the book from family to nation. As I try to suggest, the connection between body and family carries to land, and nations preside over land. This is the pattern in Israel, as its story is told in the Bible. If any nation is going to keep its memory well, it is going to have to remember itself as a land. In this context, that is, the context of the land, I am happy enough to call myself an American patriot, a mantle I do not think Stanley Hauerwas will ever comfortably wear around his shoulders. Indeed, I think Christians ought to be in this sense patriotic, partly because it will consistently put them at odds with the "patriotism"—and so also the form of "remembering"—that is so often held aloft in the modern nation state, particularly in these days after September 11, 2001.

This stance vis-à-vis the nation has been suggested to me most strongly as I have read Wendell Berry. Theologically, reading Oliver O'Donavan has also been of great help, and, I suppose, John Paul II. And Leon Kass, both in what he has said about the natural and how he has written and compiled material about family, has reminded me why Christians can never forget that they have adopted the memory of the Jews. Thinkers like these, and others who have written specifically, substantially, and theologically on memory, such as Paul Ricour or Stanley Hauerwas himself, are helping us back out of the dead-end the forgetfulness of liberalism has brought us to. With their guidance, we have good reason to hope we will recover the path.

But I have kept many of these theological and philosophical dependencies hidden in the background of this book in exchange for *stories* of family, nation, and church. Once again, most of these are drawn from or dependent upon scripture. Besides keeping the book interesting (I hope) to nontheologians, these stories help put flesh on the bones of a "political theology" that attempts to move back and forth, critically, between family, Israel, nation, and church. The scriptural dependence, I think, happily forestalls the question of what sort of sense this could make in the "pluralist" political setting of our time. If the stories are compelling, and the description of family or national life and memory apt, then the question answers itself before it is asked.

The final section of the book is meant also as its climax. The destination of human life lies beyond the fellowship of both family and nation, and settles in friendship with God. Church is more than a foretaste of this friendship; it is the friendship extended in the invitation by water and spirit, bread and wine, to partake in Christ's body. This is summed up in Jesus's phrase: "do this in remembrance of me." This phrase about church can be juxtaposed with another adapted from Genesis 3—one that might be humbly rather than harshly displayed over family and national life: "remember that you are dust and to dust you shall return." Placed together, these phrases sum up the reflections of this book. That Christians repeat them both in worship suggests, as Sam Wells is fond of saying, that God has given us all the resources we need to live well and worship God faithfully, even in the midst of so forgetful an age.

Besides those already mentioned above, others have given me help along the path of writing this book. Rodney Clapp of Brazos Press deserves special thanks since he initially encouraged me in the idea of this book, badgered me to stay at work on it, and read carefully through an earlier draft, offering suggestions that changed it for the better. Marie Gaughan, our faithful department secretary, typed in corrections and collated text files. Patty Pivirotto, our graduate assistant, checked references and watched for errors. My graduate class in Christian ethics at the University of Scranton read the book in manuscript form and offered encouragement as well as some helpful criticism. And the University of Scranton offered me needed support and time to work on the book in the form of a sabbatical leave in the fall of 2003 and a summer writing grant in 2004.

The latter meant that I spent a good chunk of time in 2004 typing away on my laptop at our summer cottage—the one mentioned more than once in this book—when I might have been out fishing or canoeing with our four children. As usual, they were understanding. They left me alone when I most needed it, while also occasionally rescuing me from my "deep thoughts" with good-hearted ridicule about practicing what I preached about memory, family, and embodiment. Robin, my wife, was especially gracious in that summer. When we married, she had no idea how many times she would need to endure the glazed eyes of a theologian who had *forgotten* what he was saying or doing because he suddenly was thinking about what next to put in some book. As if to add insult to injury, this particular book's topic is none other than how we might better *remember*. Robin's faithfulness and good humor has buoyed me up for many years, and her love has sustained me. The dedication of this book is but a small token of all that I owe to her.

Introduction

Memory Awakened

Driving into the Past

When I was just three years old, my parents purchased a cottage in Ontario, Canada. We lived near Buffalo on the American side of the Great Lakes, but my father had been raised on the Canadian side and had come to know the beauty of the lakes and forests to the north. He saved his money, seized an opportunity, and a cottage on Eagle Lake, the one with the huge fireplace made with stones that looked like petrified potatoes, became ours. Each summer our family spent most of July at the cottage, and our year was dotted with occasional weekend trips north to see the changing leaves of autumn or to hear the empty quiet of winter when the lake had iced over and wore a thick blanket of snow. That place became a part of us, although as my siblings and I grew older we visited it far less frequently.

As is the custom in America, each of us children set off to find her or his life's work, and in time all five of us lived some distance from this fixture of our childhood. I went to graduate school in the Midwest, and the only teaching position I could find when I had finished was in Arkansas, near Little Rock, a place I had never seen before arriving to take the job. While my parents had retired and were spending almost half the year at our Canadian cottage, the drive there from Little Rock was monumental, and we certainly could not afford to fly, particularly as my wife and I began to have children. Each hot summer in Arkansas I resisted a strong tug to head north. Finally, when our oldest son was perhaps five years old, he and I decided to make the trip. During that trip something awakened in me whose power I had no doubt felt before but could not name. It was the power of memory, and it is the topic of this book. I later tried to write out what had come to me along the way during this trip.

Toronto is a big city—big and getting bigger. In days past I knew it mainly as the subject in my father's chief complaint: Toronto-traffic. We had to go around Toronto to get to our cottage, hence the trouble about Toronto-traffic. Toronto-traffic was not really connected in my young mind with anything other than itself—I had no reason to make the inference from the traffic to the city. But the name was important, in that subordinate place. Our time of departure for the cottage was a great deal tied to predictions about Toronto-traffic—and there simply was no more important matter than leaving for the cottage.

Now I can see that Toronto is a very large city indeed. We need to avoid it. There are some moderately sized cities, like Birmingham, Alabama, that you might decide to pass through on the main highway. After all, bypasses add miles. Traffic might be a bit heavier, but you can average 55 mph, and if you later have occasion to tell someone that you've been through Birmingham, Alabama, it's better to have had a look at the tall buildings. There is no question on this point, however, with respect to Toronto. Definitely to be skirted. I check the map. Looks like we want Highway 407. ("*The* 407," I'm sure the Canadians say, the definite article being obligatory in Canada when referring to any road worth its weight in concrete.) A new road, I suppose. I certainly don't recall hearing its number spoken as I rode along in my parents' back seat.

My son Jody, just five, has been much less trouble than I might have guessed on this two-day trip. We have lived for the last five years near Little Rock, Arkansas, of all places. Little Rock is one of those cities where you might decide not to take the bypass. I had little sense of it before ending up there—at most only a vague recollection of the National Guard and Central High. Then one day it became my home. In my field, doctorates are available, jobs much less so. So you go where they'll take you. Or maybe where God calls. A strange idea: God calling someone to Little Rock, Arkansas. Orval Faubus calls in the National Guard, and then God calls me?

In any case, Little Rock is a fair piece from the Toronto-traffic just now surging around the two of us. Although I can't remember the 407, there is no doubt in my mind how many miles yet lie between us and our destination: 150. My father to an acquaintance: "We have a place about 150 miles north of Toronto." Or my father to me in the middle of the dreaded Toronto traffic: "Soon this will clear up, and then only 150 miles. Three hours, son, tops." Remembering about the 150 miles is heartening, as is the part about traffic clearing up. The 407 ends and we are on the 400. Traffic only moderately heavy. On this stretch you have to be on your way to somewhere other than Toronto. "Canada's Wonderland," maybe, now looming ahead on our east side. Canadian-style Disney, complete with its own version of Magic Mountain, poking up like a termite hill on a flat desert. Kids everywhere like roller coasters, as I did and my son after me. Yet we give it no further thought on this trip. Roller coasters are for your stomach, not your soul.

Wonderland behind us . . . Labatt brewery . . . Molson Concert Parkland . . . now the 400 narrows to Highway 11 (not "the 11") and suddenly: an overpowering rush of the familiar! "This town is Bracebridge, Jody. You know, when Grandpa first brought up the ski boat a cop pulled us over, saying the license on the trailer was expired. I wasn't that much older than you. He made us go to that police station, right there. I remember there was a big discussion about whether we could even go on with the boat." My tongue is loosed, as is my young son's in response, plying me to go on. "Then what happened?" Neither of us is exactly what you would call talkative, but the stories begin to tumble out now; a door in the mind is opened and words, images, perceptions begin to spill into the open ear of the five-year-old in the passenger seat.

What is it about memory that makes us want to tell it? After we tell it we don't say, "Well, I'm glad I got that off my chest!" or "Now do you understand?" After a memory is shared in conversation we don't conspire together, the teller and the hearer, to some new scheme. Nothing is really accomplished as memory is brought forth from our minds and passed on to others. Or perhaps, in another way, everything is.

Yet the journey the two of us are on is not in the mind, but rather in a car. Despite climate control, cars travel in time and space, from one place to the next, past Toronto to Bracebridge, by lakes and rivers with distinctive names and shapes, like this one: the Magnetawan. Here the densely covered highlands, verdant with white pine and northern maple, clear suddenly and plunge over granite cliffs to the moving blue of the river below. The current swirls round wooden piers where cottagers have tied their boats. In fact, it is not only my son's questions but this place that calls memory from me; not any place, but this particular one. It is different from other places that hold my life just now, some 1,300 miles south near Little Rock.

The Magnetawan River that we cross near Bracebridge is a beautiful sight, and I point out the peculiar color and shape of the granite rock to my son. Yet anyone who has traveled there will know that there are equally beautiful places near Little Rock. No doubt it helps, but it is not the beauty of a place that makes us remember it. The police station in whose parking lot I sat while my father negotiated with the Ontario police is more ugly than beautiful. But it too calls forth a story to be shared. Perhaps the word *distinctive* is more to the point. Each place is distinct from every other place, so while you can find striking cliffs near Little Rock, they differ from these ones by the Magnetawan. But there is more again than this. It is not the distinctiveness only of place but of relation, me to the place. Were I to stand before a river near Little Rock, cliffs rising behind, and miraculously the next moment to stand here by the Magnetawan, I would not tell you that the difference was only a matter of the shape of the cliffs or of the rocks composing them. This might be so for another person, for whom neither place had any function. But for me, the Magnetawan draws me in. I am, as it were, called to join it. This does not happen by my willing in my mind to remember, but merely by my being bodily present here once again, as I have not been for some years. Memory, in fact, is as much bodily as it is mental—perhaps more. We become embodied in our memories.

"Embodied memories" cannot but evoke something for Christians, for we have words like these always waiting in the back of our minds: "and the word became flesh and dwelt among us" or "on the night when he was betrayed he took bread and when he had given thanks, he broke it and said, 'This is my body which is for you. Do this in remembrance of me.'" These last words, of course, are the words of institution recited in all Orthodox, Catholic, and some Protestant churches every Sunday. Each church building into which people file or trickle, as the case may be, is in a different location from every other church. Some are beautiful, others closer to ugly, each distinctive in some way or another. To all of them, however, people come so that they might remember. To be sure, some come to be "recharged" by the pastor's fine words of advice or perhaps offer some advice of their own, solicited or no. But in its long life, perhaps the most sustained and important work the Christian church has done is, simply, to keep a certain memory alive.

Going to church to remember, even the remembering itself, is an act, and as an act it produces effect. But we do not do it for its effect. For a fee, these days one can attend a seminar in "effective memory." In its usual setting, the "business world," we take the title to mean "effective use of your faculty of memory to meet your goals." Can it be rephrased to fit the remembering Christians do when they come to church? "The effective use of your faculty of memory to . . ." do what? Something doesn't translate. Indeed, as we kneel to take the bread and drink from the cup, the body and blood that we look upon and consume, we do not do something so that we can get up and do something else, as if the two, mixed in our stomachs, might chemically react, miraculously energizing us for the coming week. Actually, something quite like the reverse begins to occur when we remember as we commune. Rather than ourselves using or directing our memories of Christ, we find that we are drawn in and carried along by them. Yet their power is not foreign; just the reverse, it remains close to us. In fact, we feel as if we are being invited to remember who we really are.

Something like this invitation is extended to me on Highway 11 north, now, of Bracebridge, on through Sundridge, turning west at the flashing light in the town of South River, population 1,100. (The number has not changed since my childhood.) The Eagle Lake Road is winding, and the patchy pavement eventually fades to gravel. Hard granite is the stuff of the local gravel; stubborn pebbles resist the crusher. Our spinning tires catch these, and they clunk sharply, distinctively, on the wheel well. I remember the sound.

The stories of past summers are put away now, as we draw within a mile of our destination. We will wait for another trip to bring them out again. We have been on the way for two days; in these final moments our waiting turns to simple anticipation. The last turn into the narrow rutted drive, instant silence beneath the wheels as the packed soil in the ruts carries us gently over our final hundred yards. It is dusk, and the headlights flash in the glass of the back door. There is activity in the cottage behind. As we pull round to park I see the door open. My mother has been waiting. I open the car door, and a familiar world of sound and smell cascades down from the green canopy overhead. Red squirrels chatter faintly, the quiet of the wood is brushed by the muted sounds of the creatures that dwell in them. White pine mixed with cedar and balsam filters the air. I turn to see my mother coming toward us, legs swinging. Her knees have been bothering her for some years now, and she has adjusted her walk. My father has emerged as well. His shoulders slope more than I remember, but he remains the man I have seen come through that door countless times before. Today, or thirty years ago, still my father coming through the cottage door.

We exchange strong hugs and all turn our attention to Jody, whose age requires it. Questions about the trip: Doesn't it feel good to stretch? And did he remember his bathing suit? Does he want to go see the lake? My father leads my son down the rough stone steps at the side of the cottage, while I stop to lift a suitcase from the trunk. Past and present merge, perhaps future as well. Memory has brought us along our way here. We have arrived, but it does not leave us. No longer confined in the bubble passing on four wheels north from Little Rock, through Toronto and 150 miles beyond, it escapes and spreads out evenly under the tall trees, surrounding this place that I have known, and been known by. We will stay here awhile.

Where the Power of Memory Lies

This recounting of a trip taken with my son to visit my parents at a well-loved but sometimes forgotten place cannot fully reveal what I shall mean in this book by the power of memory. Like any power that grips the soul, there is mystery running through the human act of remembering and all it entails in our individual and communal lives. But I hope the story of my son and my return to the summer cottage in Canada opens for us a region to investigate if we are to begin to understand where the mystery and power of memory lie. Like wisdom, memory is something passed from one generation to the next. Indeed, while not all memories are wise—some can be cruel and destructive—all wisdom comes to us by memory. Although it is not its only home, *family*, as the human structure that most carries us through time, from childhood to parenthood to old age and death, is the natural epicenter of memory. Furthermore, memory relates in curious and intricate ways to *place*, indeed, to specific places that we have come to know intimately, and to be known intimately by. We can be displaced and still keep faithful memories, but we need special help to do so. Without place we can imagine that we are timeless, one of the most insidious modern lies. That lie corresponds to its twin deception, namely that we are only minds without bodies. Intimacy with place dispatches both lies.

Besides family, two other human structures preside in one way or another over the territory of memory. For Christians, one of these is also more than a human structure, namely, the *Christian church*. It boldly tells us things about how and what we should remember. It learned to do so by mimicking its parent, Judaism. The Christian church and Judaism function in quite similar ways with respect to the keeping of memory, although typically the Jews do it better. Indeed, for the Jews the problem is often not that they do not remember well enough, but that they do so too well, for too long. We Christians might be able to teach the Jews something about forgetting, which everyone sometimes needs to do. As it stands, however, most modern Christians are so thoroughly overtaken by forgetfulness that they have paid little attention to what the Jews might teach us about remembering. Islam also has something to say about memory, as do all religions, even if this gang of three monotheisms is particularly insistent about it. In fact, religion of any sort looks silly if it is without ritual, ritual, that is, that is genuinely passed down and not made up overnight by gurus or group therapists. Religious ritual is memory in heightened and compressed form.

The insistence of the three faiths about memory has led, like a laser-guided missile, to violent explosions in the Middle East, or, better put, the Holy Land. Jews are settling the town of Hebron because they believe their mother Sarah and father Abraham were buried there—some 4,000 years ago! Hebron is where one young Jew opened fire with an Uzi in a crowded mosque a few years ago because of some strong tie he felt to this memory; and since that time many young Muslims have followed the memory of other young Muslims to their deaths, their bodies tightly strapped with bombs of their own design. We should make no mistake. The power of memory can be angry and violent.

On the violence scale, however, we must also measure forgetfulness, which typically kills without noticing—and, partly because of this, may more quickly stack up the bodies. The modern *nation-state*, which often vies with the church for control of our memories, teaches us a curious blend of memory and forgetfulness. The blend is frequently deadly. If the ties that bind us to any one particular place can be loosened enough that we forget what being and living in that place is all about, then an abstraction called "freedom" or even "America" can substitute for that place, and we will kill and die for it, as our forefathers and foremothers might once have killed or died to protect their land. A nation or country does not have to make this substitution; America does not always. "Country," after all, is about land, as Woody Guthrie knew when he first strummed out my favorite patriotic song: ". . . from the redwood forest, to the gulf stream waters, this land was made for you and me." There is no reason why Christians cannot live happily in the country called America, and love it as a country, although what they get taught at church, or might get taught, keeps, or should keep, them from saying things like "This is the greatest nation in the world." (It is no accident that this phrase works less well when "nation" is replaced by "country." Since "country" is bounded land, and we know that each land—for example, that surrounding Little Rock, Arkansas, or that rising up from the winding Magnetawan River in Ontario, Canada—has its own unique and incomparable goodness, there is no greatest country in the world.)

In this book, I will try to approach memory in relation to these points of reference: family, land, nation, and church. I am a Christian, and so I write particularly with the latter in mind. I do not think we can get our memories about land, family, or country right unless we learn through the church (or synagogue, and perhaps even mosque) to rightly worship the God who made us and continues to sustain our powers, including our powers of memory. Though church, synagogue, or mosque guide us through human life, they are not themselves human life's totality. Human beings, human communities, necessarily remember. It is something that is distinctive of us as human creatures. We will remember—so it is not so much a matter of whether to remember, but how and what. The Christian faith helps us think this through, giving room for and passing down wisdom about the primary structures, such as land or family, where memory is kept.

If remembering is distinctively and characteristically human, the fact that we live in a forgetful age should deeply concern us. We may be in danger of becoming creatures we were not meant to be. Or, more likely, we will become sickly, suffering from memory loss.

Here and there in this book I shall try to say or display what I mean by modern loss of memory. Presently, I will say something about what I do *not* mean by it, and so clarify what about memory I will *not* address in this book.

One understanding of what memory is all about is what happens in our brain when we call up, for instance, how to spell *Mississippi*. We learned this when we were young and now remember the spelling. A certain complex set of surges and jumps and firings takes place in our brains as the letters are brought in their proper sequence to the front of our minds. All of this, the jumps and firings, is part of what might be called the biology of memory. I will not be discussing it at all. By refraining from doing so, I do not mean to dismiss it. One reason for not dismissing it is the simple but powerful fact that if we did not have the brains we do, we would not be the creatures of memory that we are.

I shall assume that some very complex and mystifying things go on in our brains biologically that relate to this very human thing, or range of things, we point to with our word *memory*. After assuming this, I will leave the matter entirely. Besides that I have not the least idea of how it all really goes on, I very much doubt that the biology of memory can tell us much about the difference between what happens when I remember how to spell *Mississippi*, when I remember the birth of our first child, or when I follow the church's command on Ash Wednesday and "remember that you are dust, and to dust you shall return." It is no disrespect to biology to say that it is not its business to tell us about these differences.

I do hope to speak in some detail about why remembering that I am dust, or even remembering the birth of our first child, is essential for me as a human child of God to do, more important than remembering how to spell *Mississippi*. As I noted earlier, we live in an age of memory loss—and it is killing us. This is not to say we have forgotten how to spell, or that we have health problems with Alzheimer's disease. Again, the problem is not biological, as I hope another story will illuminate.

Keeping Your Memory While Losing It

Talking about memory loss brings to mind sad stories such as that told in the movie *The Notebook*, where Allison, the female protagonist, has forgotten in her old age her lifelong love affair with her husband, Noah. Clearly in her case something biological has gone wrong: certain jumps and firings that once occurred in her brain don't anymore, and so she has become disoriented and confused. She doesn't even recognize her husband and her children. In a touching attempt to bring her back, as if a stranger, Noah sits down to read her a story from his notebook. The story, of course, turns out to be theirs, even if she cannot remember it.

When I saw the movie I thought of my father, for his memory, his brain, failed him in something like this way. A few years after he greeted my son and me at the back door of our Ontario cottage after our long trip from Arkansas, he started to grow confused about things and people and places he should have known. He has since died, under a rather strange set of circumstances that make for a story.

As they aged, my mother and father continued to spend the bulk of the summer at the Ontario cottage, although the trips to and from it to the home of their retirement in Florida became increasingly difficult. In the summer of his eighty-seventh year, my father, whose heart as well as his memory had weakened, was simply unable to make the trip. By this time, my wife and I had moved with our four children from Arkansas to Pennsylvania, less than a half-day's drive from the cottage. My parents had been gradually passing the care of the place over to us; that particular summer we had to take over all the work (the good work—like my father before me, I take pleasure in the chores of the place). One thing we had to do that summer was relate, repeatedly, the details of my parents' situation to the host of friends and acquaintances who called or stopped by expecting to greet my mother and father. My parents' cottage has never been a getaway in the pristine wilderness; rather it has been a web of relations with neighbors, local businessmen and -women, and fellow Christians, some cottagers but also many locals, who faithfully attend a small church in the nearby town, something my parents had also done virtually every Sunday of the fifty-odd summers they spent in the Canadian north.

The next summer, despite his slipping memory, my father's health seemed somewhat improved. In his more lucid moments he expressed a desire to make the journey north, and we set the arrangements. I recall the trip I made from the cottage, where my family and I had been staying for some weeks, to collect my parents at the airport in Toronto and bring them to join us. During it, my father, who watched passively out the window from the backseat of the car, forgot for a time where we were headed, quite despite my mother's repeated promptings. Indeed, I was not sure when we arrived at the back door of the cottage whether he had the slightest idea where we were. Nonetheless, as soon as he stepped from the car onto familiar ground, he seemed to get his bearings as he greeted Ed Brooks, our longtime next door neighbor, by name, hugged his grandchildren, and walked slowly down the path that leads to an open view of the lake.

The next three weeks, the appointed span of my parents' stay, were a mix of pathos and comedy. Soon after his arrival my father forgot that he and my mother had come to be with us and assumed (as well he might have, given the history) that we were the ones who had just arrived. As we prepared in a few days to leave the two of them alone for a time, he made a heartfelt speech after dinner about how nice it had been for us to come and visit them. The speech done, he seemed to dismiss us from his mind. That evening he puzzled to my mother about what that strange man (me) was doing down on our dock that evening, and what some blonde woman (my wife) was doing there with him. Subsequently, he went early to bed and locked us all outside.

In the next couple of weeks two of my sisters came in with their families for brief stays at the cottage with my parents, and many lifelong friends came to call. My father seemed to recognize most of them, if not all. There was a special gathering in my parents' honor at the local church and my father was presented with a plate with an etching of a loon on it, to remind him of the Canadian north and to express the church community's affection and gratefulness for his long service there over so many summers. Folks seemed to know they would not be seeing him again on this earth. Soon after he had received the plate and shaken a hand or two, he forgot anything about what it represented. It became just another object in the world, like any old plate one might eat from.

When the time of their stay was at an end, my sister drove my parents to the airport and arranged assistance for them as they passed through the airport to the gate and onto the plane. Buckled securely in his seat next to my mother while other passengers filed onto the plane, my father put down his head and died. His heart simply gave out on the Boeing 737 that was to take him on his journey away from the land and water and people he had come to know so well over so many years.

Now, in our world we do not like for people to expire on airplanes. I suspect very few of the airline personnel or medical technicians who rushed to his "aid" after he slumped over with his seatbelt fastened would have smiled at what someone later quipped, namely that, so far as my father was concerned, "this plane was bound for glory." So in all honesty I must add that technically my father did not die on the plane. After repeated shockings, this brigade of experts and specialists actually succeeded in starting my father's heart, and his body was kept in a hospital bed in Toronto until my mother and sister were finally able to make their request heard that the machines be disconnected. If we edit that last bit out of the story, I want to say that my father died a death worthy of his life, *very much with his memory intact*.

This is where we arrive at an important point about memory, about its loss, about why this is not principally about the biology of memory, and about why this book about recovering our memories in a forgetful world does not have anything to say about mnemonic technique. When I say that my father died with his memory intact I don't mean that he suddenly came to clarity on the airplane while my mother held his hand. Something like this happens in *The Notebook* when Allie comes back into herself, as it were, and suddenly knows the story she has been hearing is hers and Noah's. The movie gets it right when it suggests that we help each other to remember. But it gets it wrong when it treats memory as only what each of us sees in the mind's eye as we gaze back over the details of our past.

Instead, my father's memory, like his reputation, extends beyond him to the community and the places he inhabited. To be sure, biologically he was equipped with a certain faculty of memory, one that waned in his last few years. So equipped, like almost any human being, my father could become linked tightly with community and place. This he did, habitually and faithfully, over the span of his long life. But—and here is the point—this connection, this binding through time, was in fact two-way. Memory is about lasting attachment; by it individual human lives are gathered up into a company whose life is ongoing. If we live unattached lives, as my father did not, "memory" becomes just another event in the brain. It cannot hold us, whether or not our brains are firing on all cylinders.

It is a metaphor, of course, but there is a deep sense in which the land, the lake, and the cottage—which we still keep and visit with our children during the summer months—remember him. Even now, some years later, the land's story cannot be rightly told without him in it, not merely because we recall good times when he was there but because his contact with the land is evident at every turn: the flat rocks laid out to make a pathway, clothesline strung out, trees tended, firewood stacked. Less metaphorically, the people of this land, the folks at the local church, longtime friends on our little bay of Eagle Lake, participate in my father's memory. Particularly during that last summer, as his own capacities failed, they remembered for him—which is why I want to say that he died with his memory completely intact.

Memory in this sense is (something like) a rich and textured connection between a particular human being and the past, his or her own particular past and also a larger shared past that is carried along by human communities in their journey through time. We don't see much of these communities in the story that is told in *The Notebook*, which is almost entirely about a romantic love that springs up, well, without any context or history: eternal love at first sight. The only community to which the two lovers are connected, family, fades in and out of the picture; in fact, most of its appearances oppose in some way the romantic attachment growing between Allie and Noah. Family is often portrayed as what the two young lovers must leave behind if they are to be true to love's call.

The story told in *The Notebook* is touchingly American. It is a sweet story about lost and found memories, whose telling will do little to help Americans find their own missing memories. Memory is not just about my brain, or even about my soul that might or might not recall having found its soulmate. Rather it is about communities that gather each of us up and bear us through time.

In his widely read book *Habits of the Heart*, Robert Bellah speaks at length about the trouble contemporary Americans seem to be having with rooting themselves in a coherent and purposeful life. He thinks, as I do, that without what he calls "communities of memory" we become disoriented and confused, left floating like a lost and lonely seabird on a wild and formless sea. However, Bellah's use of the term *communities of memory* does not very clearly show how these various communities might be located in patterned relationships. We wonder what could count as a community of memory. The group of guys I have played basketball with for the past five years? My graduating class from university? These kinds of communities do in one way or another depend on shared memory, which can form into a significant force. In fact, the latter is used by fund-raisers as the key hook for bringing in millions of dollars. The right kind of memory associations can tug at our heartstrings and make us reach for our wallets, as a radio station in our area knows well enough. They play music that I and others of my generation grew up listening to, and we have set our dials. As they claim, they are not just any radio station—no, rather, a community on the airwaves.

I will not be discussing communities of memory found on the airwaves. The three I will be discussing—family, nation, and church—are privileged and stand in a certain relation one to the other. As I hope to show, our lives in family and also nation rise up from the land that gives them life, and to which our bodies return at death. Naturally, these two communities hold us firmly in the grip of loyalty. Family and nation are *"givens"* for us, which we especially need in a world of so many choices and changes. Yet for Christians, church, and the memories it accents, will not allow us to remember exactly as we might prefer in family and nation. Instead it turns us by spirit to God, the source of all life, as well as its final destination.

Part I

Family

1

The Body in the Family

A Wanderer and His Old Nurse

Remembering Infancy

When he was about forty-three years old, St. Augustine decided to write out the story of his early life as *Confessions* to God. He did this from memory, of course. Some things he tells of are still vivid in his memory, including things twenty to thirty years back. For instance, he remembers a dark night in his sixteenth year when he and a group of friends stole pears from a neighbor's orchard. One detail that is especially strong for him is that he did not want the pears at all, "for once I had gathered them I threw them away, tasting only my sin and savoring that with delight" (II.VI).

In contrast to such vivid memories as these, there is another section of his life that his memory does not reach. Since it is his intention to tell us his whole life's story, at least up until his conversion to Christianity, he needs to go all the way back to the beginning, to his infancy. For instance, he comments on learning how to smile: "Later I added smiling to the things I could do, first in sleep, then awake." And then he adds this comment: "This I have from the word of others, for naturally I do not remember; in any event, I believe it for I have seen other infants do the same" (I.VI).

While it is not surprising to any of us—for we are entirely in the same boat—it is nonetheless interesting that there is part of Augustine's life, the earliest part, that is entirely shielded from his own memory. So if we are going to tell our own story from memory, we are going to have to deal with the fact that, with respect to at least some of it—our very earliest years—we are simply missing the data.

According to Augustine, we have two other sources for these data: word from others (like our parents) who were there and can remember, or *inference*. Of these he seems to prefer the second. His suggestion seems to be that babies are all pretty much alike: what happened with this one also happened with that one. Therefore, I can reasonably infer that it happened with me. There is some truth in this about human infancy, which is why infant advice books begin on surer footing than teenager advice books. Nonetheless, anyone who has had or intently cared for more than one infant will want to go only so far with this inference.

For instance, one of our four children, our only daughter, never crawled. Instead, she "bottom shuffled." It was really an extraordinary thing and cause for the greatest merriment in our family—then, as we watched, and later, as we remember. Once they become proficient, crawling babies can cover ground at a rather remarkable rate. After she had perfected her unique skill, our daughter was equally fast, although of course she looked absolutely hilarious as she lunged her body, seated upright, from side to side, one thigh and then the other bouncing like lightning across the carpet.

Our daughter believes this was part of her life, although, like Augustine, she does not remember doing it. Yet she cannot say, as he does, that she believes it "for I have seen other infants do the same." (Apparently, exclusive bottom shuffling is the pattern in perhaps one in one hundred cases, but neither I nor [I'm sure] my daughter has ever seen anything like what she did in any other baby.) In her case we can say that she has a unique and individualized story of infancy that she could not tell—indeed, she could not know about—either by means of her own memory or by Augustine's tactic of inference. Once we see this is true of her, further reflection suggests that, counter Augustine, it applies across the board.

When my wife was nursing our children, I recall being surprised by her precise observations about each one: the way this one's hair grew, that one's lips pursed, the other one's fingers splayed. Augustine, remember, was male, and he did not spend hours nursing his children. He seems to have thought about infants *in general* rather than *in particular*. Nursing mothers do not think this way. If they have more than one, they are quite clear about all kinds of differences in their children that have been with them since their very first day. They even track these differences through life, so that when some teenager's hair stands up in a peculiar way, his mother knows exactly why.

Someone might say that all this is really about a person's body, rather than mind or memory—that part that makes a person who she or he is. The Enlightenment philosopher John Locke actually argued this case at some length. As he put it, memory (by which he meant the memory each self keeps in his or her brain) and not body is the criterion for personal identity. So if you and I changed memories but kept our bodies, you would be you in my body rather than me being me with your memory. (Never be surprised by the sorts of things philosophers have thought about.)

There are lots of little logical problems with Locke's thought experiment, which the philosopher Peter Geach has pointed out with precision. But Christians can skirt the discussion. They know that Locke can't be right since, according to the Christian faith, the human person is a unity of body and soul. This means, simply, that we are our bodies, even if also more than our bodies.

The significance of this can be overlooked. It means, simply, that we can never get away from our bodies and still be ourselves. And, as our discussion about babies has made clear, from the start our bodies are actually better known by others. Indeed, if we think of ourselves really as our bodies, it becomes much clearer to us that we are the person whom our parents conceived. Put another way, there is one community we are part of simply insofar as we are bodily human beings, namely, the community of family. If family is one of Robert Bellah's communities of memory, then we are born into memory—even before we ourselves can remember.

Later on in life we might have reason to try to forget this. Or, more to the point, we might get taught to forget it by a society that wants us to think of ourselves as minds only and not as bodily members of the community of family. Subsequently in the *Confessions* Augustine speaks of the "river of custom" that sweeps all of us along, making sure that we think and behave like everyone else around us. He thinks the river took strong hold of him in his adolescence and never let go until he was in his thirties, when God plucked him out.

In our own time the "river of custom" runs strong with the current of individualism. We are taught to "be ourselves," to "strike out on our own," to "march to the beat of our own drummer." We are supposed to find a story that is ours and no one else's. The advice has the effect of making us think that we really must find ourselves separate from the communities that sustain us by their memory, of which the family is the most obvious example. So we often feel compelled to break free and go off on our own as a sign of our essential independence from these communities.

We might imagine this is something we modern people do, and ancient peoples did not. But a remarkably old and powerful story shows otherwise. It put this style of living "free and independent" under the microscope, showing us quite perceptively what can come of it. The story is by the Greek poet Homer: *The Odyssey*.

Life as a Cyclops

The Odyssey is a sort of sequel to *The Iliad*, in which we are told the story of the war between the Trojans and the Achaeans at Troy, or Ilium. In that story, Odysseus is not the great hero; rather Achilles is. Achilles is the greatest of warriors, not simply because of his unmatched fighting prowess, but because of his steely will that is moved only by the highest things: love, revenge, or honor. Moreover, Achilles will give you the truth, whether you like it or not. By contrast, Odysseus repeatedly shows himself to be one of the world's greatest liars. His great virtue is cleverness: strategy. He is the man, as Homer says, "who is never at a loss." It is not a coincidence, then, that Odysseus survives the Trojan Wars, where lives like Achilles' came to a heroic end.

If you haven't read *The Odyssey*, you may be surprised at how long it takes Homer to get to the man for whom the story is named. Instead, the first four books of the story are about the mess back at Odysseus's home, the island of Ithaca, from which he has been so noticeably absent. Since the king of Ithaca (Odysseus) has been so long delayed in returning from the Trojan War, scheming noblemen assume he is gone for good and take aim at making his beautiful wife, Penelope, their bride. They are piggish men who have slunk in to fill the void in authority in Odysseus's communities, both family and nation. Penelope is holding out, but the situation is getting desperate—and still no word of Odysseus. In a last-ditch effort, Odysseus's son Telemachus sets out to find news of his father, visiting wise men like Nestor or Menalaus, Achaean island lords like Odysseus, who sped back from the Trojan War to set their respective domains in order. Telemachus is received generously in these kingdoms and offered food and hospitality. This contrasts markedly to the state of things on Ithaca, where guests are ignored or mocked and one cannot even snatch a morsel in Odysseus's household without one of Penelope's leering suitors snarling it away.

When we finally meet Odysseus, he is pining away on the shore of a distant island for his beloved Penelope, whom he so longs to see. It all sounds quite romantic, but do not reach too quickly for the Kleenex.

First, as you get to know Odysseus, you will find it increasingly difficult to believe him. Second, this island is owned by the ravishing sea nymph Calypso, whose sexual charms are considerable. They have been enjoying one another thoroughly—for the space of a year!

At almost every turn of the story, Homer sends us this message about Odysseus: rather than a settled family man or attentive island king, Odysseus is a wanderer, an adventurer. He likes new situations, new experiences, new stimulations. This fits exactly with his cleverness and wit. He seems purposefully to get into jams, so that he can devise some new trick to get himself out. He is the man who is never at a loss.

Of course this is also what makes *The Odyssey* an interesting story. Once Odysseus shows up, the story is off and running. But before we run off with it, we must mark the point that has been made about family and political community. Odysseus's family, and his kingdom, is a mess. The reason is simple: Odysseus is not there. Why not? Because he has been off to war, and since then, off wandering, gathering adventures. This contrasts with other island kings, Menalaus or Nestor, who came home. Kings and fathers, these men show us, are supposed to keep domestic and civil order. When they do, their island homes become ordered places amid the chaos of the sea, a refuge for travelers where a meal can be shared, friendships forged, and stories told. When they do not, as Odysseus has not, their islands begin to turn wild.

If Ithaca is turning wild, there is another island in Odysseus's adventures (which we hear of from book five onward) that defines wildness. This is the island of the Cyclopes, those fierce, one-eyed giants. Odysseus visits this island early on with his ship's crew, and what happens there sets the action thenceforth.

Cyclopes, according to Homer, are not only giant one-eyed monsters; they are "louts, without a law to bless them. In ignorance leaving the fruit of the earth in mystery to the immortal gods, they neither plow nor sow by hand, nor till the ground. . . . Cyclopes have no muster and no meeting, no consolation or old tribal ways, but each one dwells in his own mountain cave dealing out rough justice to wife and child, indifferent to what the others do" (IX, 114–25).

There is no law on the Cyclopes' island but this one: "every Cyclops for himself." There is no society here, no tribal ways. Nothing is passed down; there is no shared memory. The Cyclopes' island is virtually indistinguishable from the crashing sea that surrounds it—where there is no history, only endless water. In the story this affinity is confirmed by the particular Cyclops that Odysseus and his crew meet up close and personal, Polyphemus. This brute turns out to be the son of the wild and fierce god of the sea, Poseidon. Polyphemus is a very mean and cranky fellow who, unfortunately for Odysseus and his crew, has the strength and size to back it up. He scoops up nearly the whole lot of sailors, takes them into his cave and begins to eat them, one by one. Odysseus protests, making the point that they are guests to whom proper hospitality is owed. Yet clearly here "hospitality" has no meaning. How could it, for there are no traditions? Rather, hospitality is turned on its head. Instead of offering his guests a meal, the Cyclops turns them into one!

This is one of Odysseus's toughest jams, but he is up to it. He and his men who weren't already for dinner jam a burning log into Polyphemus's one eye and sneak out of his cave, clinging to the underbellies of his sheep. Once he discovers they have escaped, the Cyclops throws a fit and comes roaring after them, even though he can't see a thing. This is when Odysseus makes the biggest mistake of his life. It is, in a way, the defining moment of the story.

When the Cyclops earlier asked Odysseus his name, he cleverly lied that it was "Nobody." Polyphemus, so dumb he doesn't get the wordplay, keeps referring to Odysseus as "Nobody" throughout their discussions. Comically, after he has lost his only eye and his human dinner, in his tantrum Polyphemus screams out to his parent Poseidon that "Nobody tricked me, Nobody ruined me!!" But as he escapes the island on his ship, quite uncharacteristically Odysseus feels compelled to tell the truth about himself. He shouts out, "Cyclops, if ever mortal man inquire how you were put to shame and blinded, tell him Odysseus, raider of cities, took your eye: Laertes' son, whose home is on Ithaca" (IX, 550).

Thinking quickly for once in his life, on the spot Polyphemus prays to Poseidon: "Oh hear me, lord, blue girdler of the islands, if I am thine indeed, and thou art father: grant that Odysseus, raider of cities, never see his home: Laertes' son, I mean, who kept his hall in Ithaca. Should destiny intend that he shall see his roof again among his family in his father land, far be that day, and dark the years between. Let him lose all his companions, and return under strange sail to bitter days at home." These last couple of sentences summarize the story of the *Odyssey*. Odysseus goes on from there to one gut-wrenching adventure after another, loses all his crew, takes forever along the way, and when he finally gets back to Ithaca, he finds it (as we know already) in lawless disarray.

But here is an interesting thing: had Odysseus stuck with his lie, had he remained "Nobody," Poseidon wouldn't have been able to get to him, and he could have sailed happily home. And so we might learn this lesson (which Odysseus actually takes well to heart): when you are wandering on the wild sea or dealing with the likes of the Cyclopes, it is best to be nobody, and to lie to keep yourself that. To which we might add this question, which relates to our topic of family: suppose you do this with success and you actually become nobody. What happens when you come home, where you are somebody, someone's son or daughter, someone's spouse or parent?

Home Is Another Strange Island

Homer will give us the answer to this question. But let us remember the terms of the story so far. Odysseus appears to want to get back to his family and his island, but he is really a wanderer at heart who seems to love every minute of his many strange and terribly dangerous adventures. The reason he is able to make it though these dangers (as others cannot) is that he is so clever—there is no one better at lying his way out of a jam. Lying, actually, may be the way to make it in the wild world of the sea, or on sea-like islands such as that of the Cyclopes, where the rule is "each one for himself." Look out for number one, trust only yourself, keep your strategy flexible and close to your chest, and may the best man win.

I hope that putting things in this way will interest us. For this is often how we talk in our current world. It is the competitive world of business and commerce, where each of us is trying to get ahead. This is an adventurous world, one where stories of individuals who beat the odds and actually made it (like Odysseus) are told excitedly. It is not, however, the world of the family. Or, put another way, if we come to learn to live in the wild world of the sea, forming there the habits we need to survive, and return to the family with these habits working well, things are going to get rather interesting.

In *The Odyssey*, the point extends beyond the family to the civil society of Ithaca. No well-functioning society can be built on distrust and deception. Islands of genuine human social and familial exchange and goodwill are what they are precisely because they are able to keep Poseidon out, to live by laws of conviviality rather than by the harsh and simple law of the wild sea. To establish such places, though, to build trust, to care for what has been passed down instead of starting all over again with each day (as an adventurer might do), one needs to settle in for the long haul. One needs to till the ground with regularity and skill, come to be bound to other human beings through time, and tend day in and day out to the intricate and subtle matters of home and hearth. In that time and ours, Odysseuses have trouble doing this.

As Homer suggests, for men like Odysseus there can be no such thing as "familiar" (note the etymological connection to *family*). As the story draws closer to its end, Odysseus is deposited on the shores of Ithaca by the Phaeacians, a generous and friendly people, who have given him his last hospitality and left him with many gifts. There on the shore

Odysseus falls sound asleep. When he awakes, this is what he sees: "The landscape then looked strange, unearthly strange to the Lord Odysseus: paths by hill and shore, glimpses of harbors, cliffs and summer trees. He stood up, rubbed his eyes, gazed at his homeland, and swore, slapping his thighs with both his palms, and then cried aloud: "What am I in for now? Whose country have I come to this time?" (XIII, 250).

The point is, of course, that the wanderer is so used to wandering that he doesn't know his own home. And so he behaves here as would a wandering stranger, lying and hiding each step of the way. When he meets a shepherd, who actually is the goddess Athena disguised, he converses with the man "with ready speech" but not with the truth. As Homer says, "he held back what he knew, weighing within himself at every step what he invented to serve his turn," and so tells the shepherd an elaborate story about how he came from another island, how his ship was blown off course, and so on . . . all thoroughly believable lies. With some disgust Athena throws off her disguise and exclaims: "You chameleon! Bottomless bag of tricks! Here in your own country would you not give your stratagems a rest or stop spellbinding for an instant?"(XIII, 373–7). The answer, funny in the story but laced underneath with a kind of sadness, is that Odysseus has become as one with his stratagems. He cannot help but cling to them even when he has now finally returned to those who know and love him.

Hiding yourself from a shepherd you don't know is one thing. But doing so from your own father who has longed for years for your return is another altogether. Here is how Homer describes Odysseus's first encounter with his father, Laertes.

> [Laertes] wore a tunic, patched and soiled, and leggings—oxhide patches, bound below his knees against the brambles; gauntlets on his hands and on his head a goatskin cowl of sorrow. This was the figure Prince Odysseus found—wasted by years, racked, bowed under grief. The son paused by a tall pear tree and wept, then inwardly debated: should he run forward and kiss his father, and pour out his tale of war, adventure and return, or should he first interrogate him, and test him? Better that way, he thought—first draw him with sharp words, trouble him. His mind made up, he walked ahead. (XXIV, 253–66)

So Odysseus concocts a new story about how he had recently come to the island and in his travels had run into a man known by the name Odysseus, how the two of them looked remarkably alike, and on and on. For this wanderer, even fathers become strangers who need to be tested, outsmarted, kept in the dark.

Homer reserves the most striking case of this clash between one kind of life—the lonely life of adventure, strategy, and hidden identities—and the other, the domestic life of love and trust, for a woman. As things transpire, Odysseus tricks his way into the queen's court, where he can better assess what to do about the suitors who are attempting to take over his kingdom. He disguises himself so well that Penelope does not recognize him—and, after all, he has been gone for twenty years. She regards him as an intriguing stranger and orders the old, faithful servant Euryclea to give him a foot bath. Yet Euryclea is Odysseus's old nurse, who knows him better than anyone, better than he knows himself. As she begins the bath, she feels a surge of the familiar and expresses it, even as the disguised Odysseus fights her off.

> "My heart within me stirs, mindful of something. Listen to what I say: strangers have come here, many through the years, but no one ever came, I swear, who seemed so like Odysseus—body, voice and limbs—as you do." Ready for this, Odysseus answered: "Old woman, that is what they say. All who have seen the two of us remark how like we are, as you yourself have said, and rightly, too." Then he kept still, while the old nurse filled up her basin glittering in firelight; she poured cold water in, then hot.
> But Lord Odysseus whirled suddenly from the fire to face the dark. The scar: he had forgotten that. She must not handle his scarred thigh, or the game was up. But when she bared her lord's leg, bending near, she knew the groove at once. (XIX, 440–59)

As a young boy, Odysseus was gored by a wild boar in the thigh, something his old nurse knew both by story and by touch. Her hands cannot lie, nor can Odysseus's body deceive. She knows he is Odysseus, with the deepest certainty.

> This was the scar the old nurse recognized; she traced it under her spread hands, then let go, and into the basin fell the lower leg making the bronze clang, sloshing the water out. Then joy and anguish seized her heart; her eyes filled with tears; her throat closed, and she whispered, with hand held out to touch his chin: "Oh yes! *You are Odysseus!* Ah, dear child! I could not see you until now—not till I knew my master's very body with my hands!" (XIX, 542–52)

But what will Odysseus do now? Embrace her? Confide in her, this one who knows and loves him so well? No. For seen as Odysseus sees, Euryclea's knowledge of his identity, a knowledge and lifelong love that he cannot control, threatens his strategy.

> Odysseus's right hand gripped the old throat; his left hand pulled her near, and in her ear he said: "Will you destroy me, nurse, who gave me milk at your own breast? Now with a hard lifetime behind I've come in the twentieth year home to my father's island. You found me out, as the

chance was given you. Be quiet: keep it from the others, else I warn you, and I mean it, too, if by my hand god brings the suitors down I'll kill you, nurse or not, when the time comes—when the time comes to kill the other women."(XIX, 557–69)

Nurse or not, Euryclea threatens the plan. Skirt her if possible; remove her if necessary. In the Cyclops's cave, or on the friendless sea, this makes a certain sort of sense. But applied here to Euryclea it turns into a kind of madness, as she points out.

> Euryclea kept her wits and answered him: "Oh, what mad words are these you let escape you! Child, you know my blood, my bones are yours; no one could whip this out of me. I'll be a woman turned to stone, iron I'll be. And let me tell you too—mind now—if god cuts down the arrogant suitors by your hand, I can report to you on all the maids, those who dishonor you, and the innocent."
>   But in response the great tactician said: "nurse, no need to tell me tales of these. I will have seen them, each one, for myself. Trust in the gods, be quiet, hold your peace." (XIX, 570–82)

Trust in the gods, Odysseus says. But what could it mean to do so if one withholds trust from all others? The theology does not hold up. In a world of Cyclopes, there is no god but Poseidon. And in a world ruled by Poseidon there is also no such thing as home or, for that matter, family, if family is necessarily a community of memory and trust.

Loyalty Embodied

There are situations, even at home, that call for strategies similar to those Odysseus is so good at. Even though he is implicated in their takeover by his long absence, it is nonetheless true that the suitors are bad men who are destroying lives. Yet Odysseus's behavior toward his old nurse, Euryclea, plainly shows that something is wrong with how this great strategist has come to see the world.

We can understand this as a kind of failure of memory. To be sure, Odysseus has no trouble recognizing Euryclea or his father, Laertes. In fact, he knows their names and can remember precise details of their lives from the past. So the problem is not with the brain that is doing the remembering. What seems to have gone wrong instead is the connection Odysseus forges between these memories and the present. What is recalled from the past has become a set of facts with no power in themselves, bits of information whose significance can be changed and molded to fit the view of things Odysseus has now come to hold, the view of the strategist. While Odysseus recognizes Euryclea, he does not really see her at all. His life of adventure and wandering has rendered him incapable of genuine knowledge of who she is.

Loyalty is a term we use to describe the crucial connection in Euryclea's long life between the past and the present. We sometimes pledge loyalty to one another, but the loyalty is not the pledge. In fact, the very reason we need to pledge it is that loyalty can be shown only through time. The pledge stands in for the loyalty yet to be worked through and lived, which is why the pledge needs to be made only once—from that point forward it can be assumed, banked on, trusted. This is where its strength lies. We are rightly suspicious of someone who constantly pledges his or her loyalty to us: perhaps this means it is weak. Similarly, we are rightly suspicious of sudden loyalties, those that spring up without warning. For loyalty takes hold in continuity with what has gone before.

The assumption built into loyalty connects yesterday with today. Things are what they were; I am to you now what I was to you then. What has passed between us in the past holds us in the present. When Euryclea addresses Odysseus as "dear child," this is what she is saying. Yet the address is lost on Odysseus. In our modern age we might expect the retort from him: "I am not your child! I am a full-fledged adult; I have become my own person!" This response, or Odysseus's more violent one (he grips her by the throat), completely misses what Euryclea has conveyed in her words. And so he misses her. No doubt he knew her once when, as a boy, he felt the strength of her loyalty. But he has lived so long by adventure and disguise that loyalty has entirely given way to strategy. The terms move in opposite directions: whereas loyalty particularizes—we cannot be loyal to anyone at all, but only to this one or that one—strategy generalizes. Strategically, Euryclea is like Polyphemus; by loyalty, she is her particular self, and nobody else.

In a modern novel we might worry that Euryclea will turn out to be a fake. Homer gives no room to this. Euryclea *is* loyal throughout the story, not only to Odysseus but to Penelope and their son, Telemachus. She is the solidest rock on the island. Since this is true, careful readers of Homer will ask not only why Odysseus cannot see this but also what might have happened had he been able to. Euryclea volunteers to assist Odysseus in meting out justice in the household. Her offer is proudly and summarily dismissed: Odysseus will do all that by himself! And so, according to the story, he does, killing all the suitors and many others in his own household. This violence occasions a civil war, one that is arrested only when the gods directly intervene. This eruption of violence makes us wonder if the "justice" Odysseus enacts upon the suitors and the house staff (most are killed) is true justice. Justice, after all, depends on particular knowledge of particular people, which is what Euryclea, and not Odysseus, is in the position of having.

If one lived on the island of the Cyclopes, perhaps he should live by the sword, by strategy and cunning. Yet Ithaca is not such a place, as the fact that Euryclea is not a Cyclops shows most clearly. But Odysseus seems to have forgotten the difference. So long a time in the world of the sea, governed by Polyphemus's father, Poseidon, has made him unable to remember as she does. She is one in whom the past holds the present, by loyalty. Memory sustains who she is. By contrast, "memory" for Odysseus is a machine to be put to work for present strategic purposes.

Is Poseidon Lord?

I suspect that the strategic view Odysseus represents is fueled by fear born in a world where Poseidon is Lord. It is a world devoid of a certain kind of hope, the kind that is rooted in loyalty and trust, rather than the (so-called) "hope" that relies on a picture of triumph, of overcoming the odds to reach the top. This fear, and lack of hope, is widespread in our time. For we live by the strategic view. Indeed, *strategy* is our byword; at every turn we are urged to have it. Make a plan—and execute! Even when we speak from the heart, what we have said is immediately subject to "spin." What was the strategy behind that particular statement? What could he have been trying to get us to do or think by saying that?

I do not think it is accidental that in our world, as in Odysseus's, adventure is our assumed highest form of pleasure. Worlds come in packages, and in the character of Odysseus, Homer has wrapped a package up carefully, one we can unwrap centuries later and recognize ourselves. If the world is filled only with Cyclopes, what more is there to do but venture forth, to pit our power and wit against others to see who is the stronger or cleverer? "Who knows?" says our form of hope. "Like Odysseus, we just might beat the odds."

To be sure, most of us are less adventurous than we care to admit. Nevertheless, even the unadventurous ones assume that the life of the adventurer is a cut above their own. And if we cannot leave home to pursue adventure, perhaps we can produce it by changing ourselves, by adopting, as Odysseus did so often, a new and different story and identity. So we try to reinvent ourselves, or, as Athena chides Odysseus, we become chameleons, changing our identities to fit our surroundings. Of course, reinventing ourselves usually also changes our surroundings, since we come to regard the loyalties of others in the home as encumbrances and so slough them off.

Yet underneath the adventure, the reinventions of self, and the "hope" of beating the odds is the nagging fear that we are fundamentally alone, alone, in fact, in Poseidon's domain. Such fear can drive us to cynicism on the one hand or sentimentality on the other. After all, sentimentality is a kind of cloaking of what we know to be false under the cover of truth or "history." Sentimentality invents a world that we wish for but know does not exist. We live in the invented world as if in a dream from which we hope we will never be awakened. (As Wendell Berry has said, sentimentality is the main work of Walt Disney Productions.) Cynics and sentimentalists are twins with slightly different dispositions, both born from the strategic view.

As I believe Homer shows us, Euryclea represents another world altogether from Odysseus. If she is real, she bears a better hope to a world of strategy, suspicion, and fear. Euryclea represents a better hope precisely because in her loyalty she teaches us that Poseidon is not the Lord of all. This is borne in how she remembers. By it she exposes the failure of Odysseus's form of remembering. And so she represents to him the person he really is, but has forgotten about, namely, the very one who once suckled at her breast or the one who received the care of others after being gored by a boar upon the thigh.

Although Euryclea is not Odysseus's mother, she clearly represents the powerful form of remembrance that characterizes families, especially mothers. Homer's description reveals much about how this remembering works. As we noted at the beginning of the chapter, the remembrance is a great deal about physical bodies, both Euryclea's and Odysseus's. Homer tells us that Euryclea is "stirred in her heart" when she first encounters the disguised Odysseus; she recognizes his "body, voice and limbs." Then of course, there is the scar on Odysseus's thigh, which she "traces with her spread hands." It is when she "knew [her] master's very body with [her] hands" that she knew with certainty that it is him. Finally, after being rebuffed by her master, her language shifts, from his body to her own. "You know my blood, my bones are yours," she says.

If we did not know the nature of the relationship between these two, we might take Homer's language in these passages to be sexual. It is the bodily language of love—which in a way is always sexual, although not always erotic, for it is about the sharing of life between two embodied persons. In both directions, Odysseus's thigh and Euryclea's bones, it goes deep. It teaches (or reminds) us that there is an "underneath" both for Euryclea *and* for Odysseus, despite his many disguises. These two, after all, have touched at the deepest part of the body, where bodily life is given and received. One does not touch like this and then forget. The touch cannot but be remembered, and in the remembering, honored.

Euryclea knows this and speaks it; Odysseus, of course, is hiding from it. In contrast to his old nurse's, Odysseus's speech is designed to draw attention away from his body. He tries to distract her or to sow doubts about what she feels with her hands. And when he knows he is found out, he "whirls to face the dark." This suggests that, even if he is in no position to acknowledge this, it is actually a mercy for Odysseus that his body speaks, rather than his tongue. His tongue, by which he has kept others in the dark, may have kept him there as well. Mercifully, his body does not lie. And mercifully, there is someone who can still hear it speak.

Besides having a deep center, the body serves as an indelible record of time. We get stamped at birth with certain features that will age but not change: the turn of a nose, wide hands, or narrow, knobby knees. Time adds on to this record, making marks on our bodies. Scars are perhaps the clearest of these marks of time. Importantly, they always connect directly to a story. Knowledge of this bodily story is a kind of power that is rooted in physical and historical truth. So it is that the power of Euryclea's familial memory can break Odysseus's disguise. It brings to him a message of hope and mercy in the midst of the darkness of his strategic world. Unfortunately, in the story there is no sign that he heeds the message.

As parents especially know, the power of memory in family is related closely to the body. It is no accident that at the most significant bodily events of our lives—when we are born, marry, or are buried—family is given privileged place. It is a key task of family to care for one another's bodies. When family does well, it extends the body through time by sharing and remembering it. So it keeps the embodied ones from becoming Cyclopes—where one's world is only one's own. In such a world we lose track of time, and of ourselves as timeful and embodied creatures. Euryclea's memory of Odysseus, kept in loyalty at home while Odysseus has wandered, offers him the one clear chance he has in this epic poem of remembering himself. Not unlike some in our own time, he may be too busy with his own pursuits to notice.

In *The Odyssey* Homer has carefully and artfully contrasted the domestic world of hearth and home with the wild world of one-eyed strangers and the crashing sea. He has shown us as well how these different worlds produce different sorts of memories and different kinds of hope. He has not, however, resolved the question about which of these worlds is the truer. In his story, rather, the two lie uneasily side by side; the terms of one do not compute with the terms of the other. By human effort and familial and social connection, Poseidon's rule may be hedged out at the island's shore. But beyond those shores, it seems to remain the true law.

If one holds to this dualistic view, perhaps the best thing to do is to make the family a "haven in a heartless world," as Christopher Lasch has turned the phrase. And, as Lasch observes, this is largely what we have done in the late-capitalist world of Western "developed" nations. Yet for Christians, who think they know something about God that Homer could not, there cannot be two Lords. While there may be a "god of this world," as St. Paul says, it is not Poseidon but rather a fallen angel created for good, whose rebellion has made him the prince of lies. The true God, Christians say, is actually the "Father of us all," which suggests that the memory patterns of the likes of Euryclea bring us much closer to the truth about who Odysseus is than his own strategic machinations.

Yet how can this God be related through family if he does not touch us in body? Here again, of course, Christians will have something to say, although it will involve quite a long and complicated story, packed, like Homer's epics, with nuance and detail. (A glimpse of this story may be gotten from such a detail as this: when Jesus Christ, whom Christians call God incarnate, stands resurrected before his followers who are having some difficulty figuring out who he really is, he says: "Put your finger here and see my hands. Reach out your hand and put it into my side. Do not doubt but believe" [John 20:27]). At present, though, we can say that the truth of the long story about the one God being the Father of all cannot but affect what we will do with familial memory. Homer has helped us see something about its texture, its tie to body and place, and to loyalty. We will need to look elsewhere to discover its scope and its rightful form.

2

Sadness in the Family

Learning from David's Regret

Being Whoever I Want to Be

During a recent stay at a hotel, TV remote in hand, I pressed "Menu" and listened attentively to a soothing, encouraging voice that asked me: "Who do you want to be?" The reason for the question, I soon discovered, was that I could "be whoever I wanted," without leaving the comfort of my hotel room. How invigorating!

Of course we do not really believe these messages that are sent to us almost every minute in our society . . . or do we? The appeal must get results in hotel rooms across the nation, selling pornographic movies to businessmen traveling from one strange place to the other. I wonder how it would sell at home: wife in room, kids occasionally trooping through. ". . . Dad, who do you want to be? You know, you can be whoever you want, without leaving the comfort of our family room."

That's the thing about family: you really can't get away from it. Family reminds us daily that we *can't* be whoever we might want to be, simply because of who we already are.

Now of course people sometimes decide they do not want to be who they are or have been—and they leave their families. The family is certainly the right place to leave if you want to get away from yourself. The problem, of course, is that it turns out to be far more difficult than we might think to get away like this. Wherever I go, there I am.

That the family is tied so closely to who we are (whether or not we want to be that person) relates to the fact that family remains our strongest natural tie to memory. The "threat" to the family we hear of often in our time is but another form of the fact we are trying to understand in this book: that we are losing our memories. We are in danger of becoming a society of Odysseuses, who practice being "Nobody" in hotel rooms across the nation, rather than in the Cyclops's cave.

Having observed this, however, we must be careful that we are not snapped back like a rubber band to a lofty defense of the family that ignores its conflicts and even its horrors. Here talk of family memories can quickly turn sentimental. Sentimental memories are censored memories: they avoid the darkness and sorrow that a truthful memory in the family must mark.

Like the voice on the hotel TV telling us that we can be whoever we want to be, we know that someone is lying to us if they tell us that their family is perfect, that everybody in it has always gotten along just beautifully. I'd even be suspicious of the Bible if that's what it said.

But of course it doesn't. Genesis, for instance, is all about family and what it carries from one generation to the next. Yet even a glance at each story tells us that while the memories that tie one family to the next also tie us to God—the God of Abraham, Isaac, and Jacob—they also carry along anger, envy, and hurt: wounds.

Think, for instance, of the relations between Joseph and his brothers. Why were they so strained? Certainly Joseph didn't help matters with his dreamy stories at breakfast, but the deeper reason for the discord was that Joseph and Benjamin were Rachel's sons, and Jacob favored Rachel over her sister Leah, the mother of most of the other boys, and so he favored Joseph—and Joseph's brothers knew it.

Introducing David

An even more poignant story is to be found in Samuel 1 and 2. Here we are told how Israel's greatest king, the one and only David, ancestor of all of Judah's royalty, including the Messiah, makes a terrible mess of his family. David is said to be a man after God's own heart (Acts 13:22), a rather frightening thought if you look at all deeply into his character, particularly in his early days. Once David became who he was, he couldn't be whoever he wanted to be. For instance, David established his kingdom by violence and bloodshed, and so he could not later become the man of peace qualified to build God a house, a fervent hope of his.

We are told this explicitly in 1 Chronicles 22:8, but a subtler narrative thread runs through the stories of 1 and 2 Samuel, where we are shown how David's violent ways and savvy political maneuverings scar his own house deeply.

After a brilliant and fascinating rise to power, which corresponds to his predecessor Saul's fall, David settles in to rule over a united Israel, which has, by God's grace and his own cunning, become a stronger nation than ever before. Yet in this time of satisfaction over a mission accomplished, David commits adultery and murder in the space of a few days, so quickly and easily he hardly notices. As the prophet Nathan tells him, this ultimately brings violence into his own household, which becomes angriest once his children mature. Son Amnon rapes daughter Tamar; another son, the fated Absalom, kills brother Amnon and revolts against father David, sending him packing from Jerusalem, the city of peace, while he has sex with his father's concubines on the rooftop for all Israel to see.

Current scandals in the British royal family pale in comparison with what happens in the family of David, this man who is allegedly after God's heart. Of course, we also are not obliged to think fondly of David's dysfunctional family relations. Yet if we stay with his story it works its way around to something else that might link David's heart to God's. After the trouble has reached its crescendo, David is able to see how the hurt suffered by his own family is tied directly to his own sins, ones he cannot undo. Sadness washes over him at the death of his son, the sort of deep sadness that can only be rooted in regret.

Regret is a form of memory peculiarly suited to the family, since in the family we are related to one another in a web of connection that does not allow us to be "individuals" who can be whoever we want to be. What one of us is or isn't (or does or doesn't do) in the family affects all of us. So, when things go wrong in our family, we are all involved, we are all in one sense or another regretfully responsible. Regret is a difficult thing to live with; in our modern setting the most common strategy we have devised to avoid doing so is to sentimentalize. "God" often helps here: God, family, and apple pie.

But the God of the scriptures is not easily sentimentalized, nor, as we have noted, are scripture's families. David's is one of a number of these unsentimentalized families. This fact, that we have these scriptural stories of families, is an important beginning point. For it opens to us the bald truth that what we wish would not occur in our families often does.

Christians say that God is able to make all things new. He is able to overcome the past. Yet overcoming what is past is something quite different from denying or obliterating it—indeed, any attempt to do either of these things is a certain guarantee that the past will not be overcome.

Instead it will loom over us or fester underneath. Bitterness, for instance, arises out of a regret that we find too great to acknowledge or bear, and so deflect the responsibility outward to whoever or whatever we can. Bitterness is regret stripped of any hope. Bitterness has lost hope, and so lost a future. Hence, it can only turn backwards, fixating on the past.

By contrast, in David's family story, which in scripture is told so truthfully, the deep and sad memory of a broken King David opens to a future as glorious as any family's on earth. From David's lineage comes the Messiah, whom Christians call Christ Jesus. It will be a long road, however, to this, including a passage through the valley of the shadow of death. One death in particular, that of David's son Absalom, finally makes clear to David how great is his own sin and failure. He regrets this, as he should. Indeed, if we understand David as the author of particular psalms, this sin is always before him. But as these psalms also suggest, the regret is held in check by David's knowledge of the God of mercy, the only god who is able to overcome a past like David's without resorting to a sentimental lie.

David Gets What He Wants

The biblical story of David begins by taking us back to his boyhood. As with Moses as a baby in the river, or Samuel as a young boy in the temple, we sense from the start that this young man is marked by God. His whole life will matter.

The story we all remember about David as a lad is his encounter with Goliath. He is kept from a crucial battle with the Philistines because he is too young but ends up winning it with a slingshot. We might think of a slingshot as a child's weapon, and it is. Yet it also signals something more profound, namely, an epic change from the bulky armor and hand-to-hand fighting tactics associated with brawny King Saul to David's new mode of striking with intelligence and from a distance. David sizes up the enemy, discerns a point of vulnerability, and aims well. It is no wonder that the day is his and not King Saul's.

The people notice this and cheer on the road home: "Saul has killed his thousands, and David his ten thousands" (1 Sam. 18:7). Jealousy springs into Saul's heart and grows quickly into obsession. He wants David dead. The latter flees to the southern wasteland, where he gathers around him a band of dirty fighters—"everyone who was in distress, and everyone who was in debt, and everyone who was discontented" (1 Sam. 22:2).

Using these men deftly in raids on Bedouin tribes, David amasses considerable wealth and power in the south. The biblical stories of this suggest that David is lucky, yes, but also may encourage this luck with a push. For instance, one day he and his band run into the wealthy but ill-tempered Nabal, who flies off with an insult. Subsequently, Nabal turns up dead, and all that he owned, including his wife, Abigail, finds its way into David's possession. Yet David is no hoarder. He and his fighting men wisely distribute the loot from their escapades to southern cities such as Hebron, where dissatisfaction with Saul's leadership already is running high.

Meanwhile, Saul's troubles have deepened. As if losing the popularity of his people to David were not enough, his own family follows suit, including his heir and oldest son, Jonathan, who helps friend David slip his father's grasp, either oblivious or uncaring about what this means for his father's and his own political fate. Saul's downward slide is so pronounced that we are not surprised when it reaches its tragic conclusion. Saul dies a lonely death defending a nation he no longer controls.

Now one might think, as did a certain unlucky Amalekite, that David would welcome news of Saul's death. This man rushes to David, reporting enthusiastically that he had a hand in Saul's final end. Here begins a pattern that we will see repeated: David kills the messenger. As he does, David pronounces emphatically (and so all can hear), "Your blood be on your head; for your own mouth has testified against you, saying, "I have killed the LORD's anointed'" (2 Sam. 1:16).

Whatever David's intention, killing the messenger and issuing in the same breath a public disclaimer of his own involvement has a highly beneficial fallout: beneficial, that is, for David. David's popularity with the people continues to rise. This is captured well in the Bible's account of David's behavior after the next crucial death, that of Abner, Saul's general. Unlike his master Saul, Abner had political intelligence. Certainly it was he who ran things in the kingdom after Saul's death, when the young and ineffective Ishbaal is installed in his father's stead. If anyone will give David trouble on his way to the throne in Israel, it will be Abner. But Abner is a marked man. For personal reasons, Joab, David's general, hates Abner. Acting as if he had a secret to tell, Joab pulls Abner aside and runs him through with a knife. Here is how David reacts:

> Afterward, when David heard of it, he said, "I and my kingdom are forever guiltless before the LORD for the blood of Abner son of Ner. May the guilt fall on the head of Joab . . ." Then David said to Joab and to all the people who were with him, "Tear your clothes, and put on sackcloth, and mourn over Abner." And King David followed the bier. . . . [He] lifted up his voice and wept at the grave of Abner, and all the people wept . . . [Later] all the people came to persuade David to eat something while it was still day; but David swore, saying, "So may God do to me, and more, if I taste bread or

anything else before the sun goes down!" *All the people took notice of it,*
and it pleased them; just as everything the king did pleased all the people.
(2 Sam. 3:28–36, italics added)

This passage makes plain that David is able to make significant
political gains just at the time others are being lowered into the grave.
A Machiavellian observer might think these gains are no accident and
that David's tears are well planned. But the people do not think this.
They are with David all the way.

David has almost reached Israel's throne. Yet one final death is necessary: that of Ishbaal, Saul's remaining son, now quaking with fear
in Israel's throne. Two ambitious young men sneak in on him while he
is napping and remove his head. They bear it quickly to David, proud
of their part in removing the last obstacle in David's ascent to Israel's
throne. Yet they are in for a surprise, involving not Ishbaal's body parts
but rather their own. At David's command they are killed, their hands and
feet removed, and their bodies hung by the water source in Hebron for
all to see (2 Sam. 4:12). After properly mourning Ishbaal's death, David
moves swiftly from his place as rival king in Hebron over the dissent-
ing southern tribes, to take Saul's spot atop all of Israel. He brilliantly
consolidates all authority and power over the tribes and shifts attention
from the troubled past to the promising future in the newly conquered
city of Jebus, which David renames Jerusalem, the city of peace.

David's rise is meteoric. Its swiftness and completeness, coupled with
its high body count, opens it to a variety of interpretations, not all com-
plimentary to David. Put in the most minimal terms, there is a strong
tendency for the good things others possess to come surprisingly into
David's possession. Moreover, people who stand in the way of David's
advance toward greater power and glory have a strong tendency to end
up dead. And finally, when these people end up dead, others associated
with these deaths should beware, for they will have a strong tendency
to bear the blame.

Perhaps we should be learning something about David through these
accounts. A man named Shimei, a loyalist to Saul's household, thinks
the lesson is clear. Coming upon David much later in his reign in the
midst of his trouble with his son Absalom, the man shouts, red-faced:
"Out! Out! Murderer! Scoundrel! The LORD has avenged on all of you the
blood of the house of Saul, in whose place you have reigned. . . . you are
a man of blood" (2 Sam. 16:7–8).

We can see why Shimei thinks this is the right lesson to learn about
David. Yet let us not go so far. Here is what I think the scriptures have so
far clearly shown us about David: *whatever David wants, he has a strong*
tendency to get. Shimei thinks he knows why David gets what David wants:

he is a monstrous, murderous mastermind. Now, no one can carefully read through David's story and think he is anything less than a political genius, gifted with extraordinary instinct, poise, and savvy. But these can also be gathered, as the Bible tends to gather them, simply under God's smile rather than under David's malevolence. David was greatly blessed, and in the end his blessing meant blessing for Israel.

If we avoid Shimei's rush to interpret David as a monster, we will be much better able to understand the rest of David's story in 2 Samuel, which is almost entirely about his sad life with his family. Likewise, we will be better able ourselves to enter into what he learns, especially about family life and memory.

In fact, many of us in modern America also could be said to have a strong tendency to get what we want. This grows into us, and becomes our habit of seeing the world. I discovered this about myself on a recent trip to Africa. My wife and I stayed for some days with friends in a remote section of Uganda where there is no running water, no electricity, no phone line, no mass transportation of goods, etc. How did we get anything done at all? Well, surely we did: meals were prepared, gatherings were arranged, and we traveled about from place to place. Of course sometimes we ate very late; or we planned to meet but didn't; or we simply stopped along the way when the roads were impassable or night had fallen. This is where I noticed a difference in attitude. By old habit, I found that I expected things to happen as I planned, and was displeased if they didn't. My African friends, however, did not really greet each day with "expectation" in my sense; and when in its course good things came to be—for instance, when we sat down together to eat—rather than speak with self-satisfaction about all that had been accomplished, they mainly were filled with thankfulness and joy. My world, in a way, was made up of my own wishes. Theirs, on the other hand, was the world into which they had been placed, by a gracious God. They received it, thankfully, while I plotted my next move to change it for what I thought was the better.

I think David was more like me than like my African friends. Securely positioned atop the kingdom he himself had constructed, David understandably settled into the habit of living in a world where all things went his way. As you might guess, this is exactly when they begin to go otherwise. And, not surprisingly, this happens in David's family. The family, in fact, is where men and women have from the beginning been taught the limits of their powers. If anyone thinks he has the world entirely under control, let him look to his family. It will show him very quickly how thoroughly he has deceived himself.

The family is not a project we can plan, execute, and complete. Nevertheless, in our time and culture, this is how we are being taught to think of it. How to raise the smartest kids . . . how to turn out the best athletes . . . how to organize the household. If the family is approached as a project, it is bound to fail. What do we do when failure comes? Try, try again. But this is only more of the same. To see another way, we must hear the rest of the story of David.

Trouble in the Family

The pivotal story that shows us how fully David is immersed in the *what-David-wants-he-gets* world begins in beautifully understated prose.

> It happened, late one afternoon, when David arose from his couch and was walking about on the roof of the king's house, that he saw from the roof a woman bathing; the woman was very beautiful. David sent someone to inquire about the woman. It was reported, "This is Bathsheba daughter of Eliam, the wife of Uriah the Hittite." So David sent some messengers to get her, and she came to him, and he lay with her. (2 Sam. 11:2–4)

Of course as the story unfolds complications arise: Bathsheba gets pregnant, her husband, Uriah, is away fighting David's war, Uriah turns out to be extremely loyal and won't take the chances his king offers him to go off duty, and so on. But these are minor sorts of obstacles for a man who can work a plan like David, and within a short time Uriah is dead and Bathsheba is back in David's bed.

This is when God decides to speak, through the mouth of Nathan the prophet. First, he tells David a story of a rich man who serves up his poor neighbor's only lamb as shish kebabs at a party for his guests. David is indignant at such abuse of power, and wants the rich man found and strung up. This is when Nathan points out to David, "You are the man!" Then Nathan adds this curse: "Now therefore the sword shall never depart from your house, for you have despised me, and have taken the wife of Uriah the Hittite to be your wife. Thus says the LORD: I will raise up trouble against you from within your own house" (2 Sam. 12:7, 10–11).

According to the story, Nathan's daring pronouncements arrest David, and he confesses that he has sinned. Yet the next story in sequence makes us wonder about whether the confession takes up any secure home in David's life. Bathsheba's infant becomes seriously ill, and David prays and pleads and fasts and throws himself on the ground, apparently deeply affected by so sad a thing. Yet after the baby dies, he hops up and has a healthy meal. His servants are puzzled, but David says to them, in his matter-of-fact way, "While the child was still alive, I fasted and wept;

for I said, 'Who knows? The LORD may be gracious to me, and the child may live.' But now he is dead; why should I fast? Can I bring him back again?" (2 Sam. 12:22–23).

What can we say to such a response? In one sense it endears us to David. While it is true that he tends to get what he wants, David is hardly spoiled. He does not cry over spilled milk. Not everything works out as you might hope, but if it doesn't, you might as well get on with it—maybe the next time it will. Yet David's realism makes us wonder whether he has really heard Nathan's prophetic word. For the implication of David's comment seems to be that all the breast-beating and fasting of the days before were in fact a kind of maneuver. He was working on the world, or God, to get something he wanted. No doubt, this is the attitude or posture that thus far has garnered David such success. But is it not also the same posture and display that so impressed the people at the time of Abner's death? The same attitude that left Uriah dead?

The difference between this little story and earlier ones is not a changed David but a changed setting, from national politics to David's family life. Yet Nathan has warned us that David will face not just a few glitches in his plans but tragic failure. And so it begins to happen. David's son Amnon is sexually attracted to David's daughter Tamar, his half-sister, and acts on it. Not only does he rape her, the Bible reports that immediately afterward he loathes her and drives her from his bedroom. Absalom, Tamar's full brother, Amnon's half-brother, is justifiably angry, not only because Amnon did what he did but also because his father, David, ignored the whole thing, being partial to Amnon, his firstborn. As Absalom's smoldering anger toward Amnon turns to hatred, he begins to plot—something he turns out to be good at, not unlike his father. Indeed, in an opening skirmish of wits between father and son, Absalom proves wilier and gets his revenge: Amnon is killed by Absalom's servants.

Like David who took cover from Saul among the Philistines, Absalom knows the safest place to flee from the king of Israel is among his enemies. After Amnon's death he flees to Geshur, where he stays with the king. Yet Absalom does not mean to leave home, like a young man who strikes off from his father's house in disgust, hoping for a better deal in another land. Israel and its people remain in his sights. He returns to Jerusalem, where he uses his beauty, charm, and princely position to endear himself to his countrymen. As the Bible reports, "Whenever people came near to do obeisance to him, he would put out his hand and take hold of them, and kiss them. Thus Absalom did to every Israelite who came to the king for judgment; so Absalom stole the hearts of the people of Israel" (2 Sam. 15:5–6).

There are shadows in Absalom that we do not find in David, a brooding and seething that find design and reason for revenge behind misfortunes, ones that David could accept, as he accepts the death of Bathsheba's firstborn. Otherwise, however, the similarities between father and son are striking. Absalom came from David, not only through his loins but also through his actions and habits, from his sins. God's punishments spoken by Nathan the prophet are not arbitrary. The hatred and violence, the destruction, that run through David's family life follow by a dark but inexorable logic from David's own earlier life. There by habit he used power, popularity, and position to get what he wanted, even if this meant the death of many men and destruction of many families, Uriah's and Bathsheba's among them. Now it falls back upon him in the form of a much beloved son, made in his own image.

The popular song "Cat's in the Cradle" by Harry Chapin follows such a theme: a father with no time for his son turns out a son with no time for his father. At the song's conclusion, the father understands. "My boy was just like me," he sings. Yet he can do nothing with his understanding. It sits in his heart as a deep yearning yet in quiet regret, as the father-son relation moves on through time, broken and incomplete.

Family Trouble Becomes Tragedy

In the early days of Absalom's rebellion, this is David's position: he yearns and regrets. Absalom has become who he is, and David can do little about it but wish for something else. "David mourned for his son day after day. Absalom, having fled to Geshur, stayed there three years. And the heart of the king went out, yearning for Absalom; for he was now consoled over the death of Amnon" (2 Sam. 13:37–39). But this quiet regret is destined to mount to a shattering conclusion after Absalom goes south, where he, again following the footsteps of his father, is crowned as a rival king in Hebron and advances with an army to capture Jerusalem. David and his forces are forced to flee.

His back against the wall, David regains the strategic skills of earlier years and lays out a battle plan that will work. Yet his mind is divided, for his opponent is now his son. Before the battle he pleads with Joab and his other generals: "Deal gently for my sake with the young man Absalom" (2 Sam. 18:5). Yet Joab is a veteran fighter who believes, as David once believed about Uriah (and possibly also about Saul, Abner, Ishbaal, and many others), that rivals are much better off dead. Finding Absalom hanging from a tree, entangled in his own lovely locks, Joab runs him through with three spears (18:14).

Knowing of Absalom's death before David does, readers of the biblical text can only wait with anxious anticipation to see how he will receive the news of it. Will David please the people with a glorious display of tears? Will he remind everyone that Joab, not the innocent David, is the man with blood on his hands? Will the messengers bearing the news of the death of a rival join him in the grave? Will David strengthen himself, wash his face, and sit down to dinner, knowing that he did what he could to save his son's life, and that it is now time to get back to the business of the day?

The answer, of course, is none of the above. For David has been changed by the sadness and regret his family life has carried him through. As the Bible relates the story, David sits by the gates of Mahanaim, a city in Gilead, awaiting tidings of the battle. Messengers appear in the distance, two of them, running to bring the news. The one named Ahimaaz arrives first.

> He prostrated himself before the king with his face to the ground, and said, "Blessed be the LORD your God, who has delivered up the men who raised their hand against my lord the king." The king said, "Is it well with the young man Absalom?" Ahimaaz answered, "When Joab sent your servant, I saw a great tumult, but I do not know what it was." The king said, "Turn aside, and stand here." So he turned aside, and stood still.
>
> Then the Cushite came; and the Cushite said, "Good tidings for my lord the king! For the LORD has vindicated you this day, delivering you from the power of all who rose up against you." The king said to the Cushite, "Is it well with the young man Absalom?" The Cushite answered, "May the enemies of my lord the king, and all who rise up to do you harm, be like that young man."
>
> The king was deeply moved, and went up to the chamber over the gate, and wept; and as he went, he said, "O my son Absalom, my son, my son Absalom! Would I had died instead of you, O Absalom, my son, my son!" (2 Sam. 18:28–33)

I cannot read this passage with dry eyes. Here is a man whose brilliant rise to Israel's throne and his subsequent ordering of its national affairs exceeds by far any other political achievement in Israelite history. So mighty and gifted is he that nothing has eluded his grasp—nothing, that is, but what he evidently in this passage wants so desperately: for his son to be alive, for love to hold between them, for his family to be whole. This he cannot and will not have. It is gone from him now, lost forever. And so grief seems to swallow him up.

Because this passage echoes former ones when news of a death is brought to David (here with quite different results), and because father and son's stories have followed such parallel lines, we are able to see a peculiar element in David's grief. He mourns not just because Absalom is lost, but because his loss, David knows, is tied tightly to his own attitudes and actions. He wants them back, so he can get his son back.

He wants to restore what his own sin has destroyed. But of course this he cannot do.

As we have noted, the family is the strongest natural tie to memory. As we also noted, the family reminds each of us that we cannot be whoever we want to be. And the reason is that in the family, we already are who we are. In David's story we are brought face to face with a form of memory that combines these points: we wish things were different, but we know they cannot be. This is the space in the family that fills with sadness and regret, which David feels so deeply.

The space in the family for regret is far wider than in any other community, such as country, church, or neighborhood. This is because, more than these, our families are what they are because we are in them. For instance, we can easily imagine our countries or even our churches going on pretty much as they are without us in them. By contrast, we are locked into the family, and it is locked to us. We shape it by being whoever we are. We affect it, even if we try not to by neglecting or ignoring or leaving it.

This closeness in the family means that our misdeeds will not easily fade away. In a broader theater like "nation" we come more easily to an overall appraisal. The Israel that David built, sometimes in quite violent and coercive ways, flourished during and after David's reign. A few men were unjustly killed, but on balance he made it a much better and stronger community. Yet this is not typically how we talk about our role in the family. We don't say "in the broad scope of things, he was a good father." Instead we think of specific failings, this infidelity or that burst of anger. The family will not let us forget such things, and, as a family member, we will remind ourselves. This is why memories that have turned to regret in the family are so nagging and disturbing. We are constantly reminded by the presence of the other what did not work out, and so also of how we contributed to this by our own sins.

It is not only the presence of family members that presents our failing to us, but their absence, especially if it is due to a premature death. Indeed, even if our actions or inactions were not evidently connected to such a death, we nonetheless feel as if they were, and we count them as sins. "Why did I give him the keys to the car that day?" one parent wonders. "Why didn't I give her a call on that day she seemed so sad?" asks another.

David feels this absence as he weeps in the chamber over the gate. He longs for his son who is dead, for a relationship with him that never was, even perhaps for another David who would have lived differently from the real David and died in the stead of his son. But he can have none of these things and so is overcome by the deepest regret.

What should David do with this regret? We are tempted to say that he ought to live with it for awhile; perhaps it will bring him to some awareness of how Uriah's mother or father once felt. We do not want him to forget, as he seemed to earlier, dusting himself off after receiving the news of the death of Bathsheba's firstborn. Yet from the sadness conveyed in this biblical text and from what we know otherwise of regret in families, those who regret like David do not need to be told to remember. Indeed, telling them to forget is useless, for this would be like forgetting themselves.

God's Merciful Forgetfulness

"Forgetfulness" is something David appropriately prays for in another section of the Bible, not that he would forget, but that God would do so. This kind of forgetfulness is possible only given a certain sort of god. That there is such a god may be the only basis on which one can go on without being destroyed by the regret felt after a life such as David's and a death such as Absalom's—a pattern of life and death that I suspect is more common than we might guess. Here is what David prays:

> Be mindful of your mercy, O Lord, and of your steadfast love,
>   for they have been from of old.
> Do not remember the sins of my youth or my transgressions;
>   according to your steadfast love remember me,
>   for your goodness' sake, O Lord! (Ps. 25:6–7 NRSV)

We might imagine that David wrote these words while thinking of Absalom and how he had failed him as his father. What does he want forgotten, and what remembered? He, David, will not forget the sins of his youth, but he hopes God will. Moreover, David wants to be remembered by God in a way that David cannot remember himself, namely, according to God's steadfast love. His fervent hope is that God's remembrance of David not be guided and defined by David's sins, but rather by God's mercy, which is from of old.

The remedy for the deep regret that arises so often in family life is not the forgetfulness of the one who regrets, but rather remembrance on the part of another whose nature is mercy. This memory is not guided by our sins, but by God's mercy and love. In one sense the sin remains—it is always before our eyes. Its effects cannot and will not be removed from the world: in this world, David will not see Absalom again, Uriah will never be a father, Saul and Jonathan will never be reconciled. Yet the hope for David, the consolation, lies in that the God who created the world will not remember his creatures in the light of their failings. The "forgetfulness" of such a God opens up the possibility for his creatures that we may take up other forms of memory besides regret: joy, gladness, song, and praise.

These new possibilities are told in another psalm attributed to David, Psalm 51, one of his best known. At its beginning David makes it clear that he cannot and will not forget his own transgression. Yet it turns out to be a great benefit to David that his sin was not only against Absalom or Tamar, Bathsheba or Uriah, but against a God whose property is always to have mercy. So David can hope for a "blotting out," that his life after the sin be controlled neither by his sin, nor its effects, nor his regret over them both, but rather by a new and right spirit that comes to him from outside of him.

Read in the light of David's life, the psalm powerfully demonstrates why we can say that his heart was like God's. The stories of David's life told to us in the Bible might push sometimes toward Shimei's assessment of his character. We should not forget these stories. But for David and others like him (perhaps this means all of us), the Bible continually shows that sin and regret over our sinful past need not be the last word.

> Have mercy on me, O God,
>   according to your steadfast love;
> according to your abundant mercy
>   blot out my transgressions.
> Wash me thoroughly from my iniquity
>   and cleanse me from my sin.
>
> For I know my transgressions,
>   and my sin is ever before me.
> Against you, you alone, have I sinned
>   and done what is evil in your sight,
> so that you are justified in your sentence
>   and blameless when you pass judgment.
> Indeed, I was born guilty,
>   a sinner when my mother conceived me.
>
> You desire truth in the inward being;
>   therefore teach me wisdom in my secret heart.
> Purge me with hyssop, and I shall be clean;
>   wash me, and I shall be whiter than snow.
> Let me hear joy and gladness;
>   let the bones that you have crushed rejoice.
> Hide your face from my sins,
>   and blot out all my iniquities.
>
> Create in me a clean heart, O God,
>   and put a new and right spirit within me.

Do not cast me away from your presence
    and do not take your holy spirit from me.
Restore to me the joy of your salvation
    and sustain in me a willing spirit.

Then I will teach transgressors your ways,
    and sinners will return to you.
Deliver me from bloodshed, O God,
    O God of my salvation,
    and my tongue will sing aloud of your deliverance.

O Lord, open my lips,
    and my mouth will declare your praise. (Ps. 51:1–15)

It is interesting to compare David's words with Odysseus's. As the latter encountered his old nurse, he used words like weapons to cover his body, to hide the remembered truth about himself. But Euryclea touches him deep in his thigh and remembers. David here, like the prophet Isaiah, needs his lips cleansed so that he might speak the truth. This occurs only as his body is crushed and his sins forgotten—at least by God.

Odysseus and David are similar sorts of men. Both are mighty men of violence, full of vigor and practical intelligence. Each is blessed with an extraordinary share of good luck, and from each one's tongue words flow smoothly and convincingly. For both men, strategizing is second nature. These are extraordinary gifts, and rare. Each is positioned to benefit his people a great deal.

Of course Odysseus is mythic, and David historical. Nevertheless, the divergence between each man's story, after the similarity, is instructive. Despite his abuse of Uriah, David is the better servant of his people. In the Odyssey we never really get a chance to see Odysseus rule—which makes us suspect Homer doubts that he can. Yet the deeper and more telling difference is that David, as opposed to Odysseus, can be broken. The hardened habits of success and the almost impermeable shield of strategy somehow do not protect David from seeing the truth about himself. As we see him weep for his son at the city gate we know that his heart has opened and that he sees himself as he really is.

What accounts for the difference? It may be less from inside, more from the context in which each life is lived. And the context is theological. As I have suggested, Odysseus has lived in Poseidon's world long enough that it has become the only world he knows. Even when he reaches Ithaca, his "home," Odysseus continues to live as if Poseidon were Lord. David's god, by contrast, is the God of Israel. The God of Israel punishes, as Poseidon might be thought to, but he does so as a father. As such, David can throw himself upon him and open to him his "secret heart." This secret place is sealed, unless trust can penetrate it. Trust is related to Euryclea's loyalty but also exceeds it, since it is based not merely on constancy through extended absence, but upon love in the face of failure and sin.

To be rightly remembered, ironically, sin requires a certain kind of forgetfulness. This is because, as we have seen, its weight is too heavy to bear. Weeping at the city gate, David bears this weight over Absalom. His beloved son is dead, and he knows it is no one's fault but his own. Yet Psalm 51 opens to the idea that David can carry his load of regret to God, the God he has learned (as an Israelite) to trust. He gives God the burden and asks him to "forget"—which is, in effect, to bear the world along as if it did not have David's sin in it. David needs this; by the use of his power and great strategies he has made a world in which his son is now dead. David cannot but live in that world. He will not forget his sin. But if the sin does not determine the world, if the world is instead determined by a gracious God in whom we can confidently place our trust, then David can perhaps find the strength to go on.

The function, in other words, of God's "forgetting" is that, in the world of God's forgetfulness, one not determined by David's sin, David can go on even as he truthfully remembers the sadness that has come as a result of his own failings. For this to occur David must leave his strategies behind—something his counterpart Odysseus never does. For David a second step follows, one that Odysseus never even approaches. He carries his failings to God. Regret carried to the right sort of god, confessed as sin, can open to forgiveness. As opposed to his own constructed world of power and strategy, in the world ruled by the God of mercy (and not Poseidon), David can find sufficient hope to go on in joy and truth.

3

Redemption Comes to the Family

Blame in the Family

Only an insensitive reader would say of David as he weeps over the death of his son Absalom that it "served him right." Mind you, if the story of David were used solely to adduce evidence for a trial on that point, the prosecution might win the case. In his relationship with his son and his nation, David did (or failed to do) many things that contributed significantly to Absalom's sad end. Yet when we hear David cry "My son Absalom! My son, my son Absalom!" we do not think much about blame.

The art of the biblical narrative keeps us from rushing to this judgment. If we have read well, we know David is not only a seducer of Bathsheba and a murderer of Uriah, but also a leader of men and a lover of God. But it is not merely that. For no matter what we think of David, when he weeps here as a father over his lost son, we cannot but feel sadness, not only *for* him but *with* him. Grief in the family evokes sympathy in all of us, as well as a looming sense of our own relation to tragedy. It could be my father or mother weeping, or me.

Tragedians have long known that the family is their most productive subject. Think here of Oedipus, Antigone, Hecuba, or Lear. These characters move us, as they have moved so many for so long, because we know the truth that tragedy in our own families is always only a step or two away. By contrast, the "family values" champions of today appear somewhat desperate—almost as if they hope continual talk of "strong" families will save their own from trouble. It never does, of course. We are spared from tragedy in our families only by God's grace.

This is why we know better than to make much of the distinctions between a family whose tragedy has come from accident or illness and those, like David's, whose have come from rebellion and neglect. Hearts break in either case, perhaps even more deeply in the latter. Whatever our sins, we did not mean for them to destroy our family.

Ironically, the sense that we should not make much of who's to blame in another's family tragedy reverses itself within our own families, where blame arises almost at every turn. There is more than enough to go around. Frequently it is reflexive: everyone involved in the family in some way blames herself: "Oh, if only I hadn't said this, or done that." "If only I had noticed or listened." The close proximity of all the family members to sadness endured, their necessary share in it, seems to override individual agency. What would we make of a family member who stood up and said, "I had nothing whatsoever to do with this sad thing that came our way"? Saying such a thing is an affront to the family, even a kind of act of secession, since underneath it seems to imply that I am not one of you.

I suspect this blame cannot be absolved, or family tragedies healed or made right, within the family itself. Something new must come to pass over it; a fresh wind must blow over the parched and broken earth.

The function of memory in the family relates to this point, more on the wounded side than the healed. For it is often the memory that holds the blame and guilt; it needs to be washed by grace. We might think of this as a need to *forget* or to let go of a memory of sadness and pain that in the family has fused with guilt. As we have noted, the psalms often use this language of forgetting: God's of our sin.

Losing and Finding

The language of "losing and finding" may better suit memory in the family than the language of blame. At Absalom's death, David suffers loss almost too deep to bear. In such a case the memory is tempted by the prospect of holding onto what was lost. We can think here of the bedroom that a mother whose daughter has been tragically killed keeps in exactly the same condition for years. The empty room is a fitting image. For what is kept is not the person loved, but rather her lostness. She cannot be found in the room.

The language of "lost and found" reminds us of stories Jesus told. In Luke he builds a series of three parables around the terms: the lost sheep, the lost coin, and the lost or prodigal son. In none of these cases is Jesus at all concerned about whose fault it was that the thing got lost. Did the sheep wander off because the shepherd was inattentive? Did the woman misplace the coin? Did the father fail in some way in the raising of the younger son? Perhaps. But for the stories, none of that matters. They are also more about finding than losing. Finding makes no sense without loss, but when it arrives, finding trumps losing any day of the week.

It is interesting that of the three parables about losing and finding, the one about family is the least well resolved. For instance, the woman who has found the coin throws a party with her friends, and they all come to rejoice (Luke 15:9)—and so the parable ends on an up note. The prodigal's father also throws a party to celebrate what was found. But here things do not go so easily, for family memories intrude. The older brother refuses to go. He says to his father: "Listen! For all these years I have been working like a slave for you, and I have never disobeyed your command; yet you have never given me even a young goat so that I might celebrate with my friends. But when this son of yours came back, who has devoured your property with prostitutes, you killed the fatted calf for him!" (15:29–30).

Almost every one of the older brother's words is laced with complaint. He has turned sour. Yet, as everyone who reads this story for the first time feels, he has a point. And the reason he has a point is that the story takes place in the family, where, we all think, new beginnings are not really possible. By nature, families are governed by the past. As we have noted in the previous two chapters, this is their key strength. Exceeding all other communities, families carry us bodily through time. So they anchor us and keep us from becoming lonely wanderers in Poseidon's unfriendly sea.

The Christian gospel is about redemption, about rebirth. The family by itself does not offer this. To contrast the three "lost" stories again, to the first two Jesus adds this conclusion: "Just so, I tell you, there will be more joy in heaven over one sinner who repents" (15:7). Yet no such conclusion is offered in the case of the family. The father tells the older son why he should rejoice over his brother's return, but that is all. We are not told that he took the advice and actually rejoiced. Indeed, the strength of his complaint suggests to us that he did not. The joy is thus incomplete, unresolved. This is especially troubling, since of the three parables we are quickest to think of God when we read this one: God is like the father. But precisely here the forgiveness and new beginning that is offered doesn't entirely take. The family, it seems, may resist redemption. And the reason is memory.

It is therefore tempting to throw the family out when it comes to redemption, to make salvation entirely about individuals and their personal relation to God. This theological position has characterized our modern world, the same modern world that has turned out to be so good at producing Odysseuses, wanderers for whom "home" is just another strange island. Recognizing the trouble in this, some postmodern theologians have made redemption wider and more corporate, accenting the significance of church, the new family of God.

The change is for the better, yet we cannot but feel a nagging artificiality in all the church talk, particularly if we go to one regularly. Something is missing in the middle where we live out our lives in real families and real churches. In this postmodern redemption, the church seems to drop down upon us from out of the blue, unmediated through the bodies we inhabit, formed as they are in and through the family. Nature and grace do not meet, nor do the memories and stories that carry them both.

Can Families Be Redeemed?

When I was growing up in the evangelical world of individual redemption, where, nonetheless, we read the Bible almost unceasingly, I had, I remember, some questions about the story in the Acts of the Apostles where Paul and Silas are asked by the desperate jailer in Philippi what he must do to be saved. They say: "Believe on the Lord Jesus, and you will be saved, and your household" (Acts 16:31). So, I wondered, how could the father's belief save his kids—who I assumed were part of the "household"? (Actually, I wondered if there might be some promise in this, since I was far more confident that my father and mother "believed" than that I did.) But there it was in the text, twice—the jailer did what he was told, and so "he and his entire family were baptized without delay" (16:33).

The implication of the story is that grace, redemption, *can* come to the family. This is important not only to counter the individualist who imagines that it's all only about me and God, but also those who read the gospel as requiring a necessary break with the family. The latter have a strong biblical case: many of the comments Jesus makes about family are not the sort pro-family advocates would list on their web site. "Whoever comes to me and does not hate father and mother, wife and children, brothers and sisters, yes, and even life itself, cannot be my disciple" (Luke 14:26).

Jesus's spin on family, and the interjection of a church that draws us all up into the family of God, did make a significant difference in how Christians viewed the family. Unlike the Roman (and also Jewish) world with which they interacted, the earliest churches did not think that marrying and having children was a requirement for all good Christians. As Karl Barth has put it,

> In the sphere of the New Testament message, there is no necessity, no general command to continue the human race as such and therefore to procreate children. . . . On the contrary, it is one of the consolations of the coming kingdom and expiring time that the burden of the postulate that we should and must bear children, heirs of our blood and name and honour and wealth, that the pressure and bitterness and tension of this question, if not the question itself, is removed from us by the fact that the Son on whose birth alone everything seriously and ultimately depended has now been born and has now become our Brother. (*Dogmatics* III/4, 265)

The necessity, the burden, the pressure, that is removed here involves where we are headed rather than where we come from. So does redemption. We come from natural families, but we move beyond them into God's family of the church. So redemption is about the future, the new future the church opens to us in the new family of God.

The existence of a new family that transcends the natural family suggests that the redemption of the natural family is not a necessity: you can be saved even if your family is not. Nevertheless, knowing what we do about God's redemption—that it is bodily and not merely spiritual, that it is corporate and communal as well as individual and personal, that it reaches infinitely far, into all the corners of human life (for example, into the family of the jailer in Philippi)—we also cannot exclude the family from redemption.

It seems to me that the parable of the prodigal son deposits us where we need to be about the family and redemption. We simply don't know how the older brother will behave after his father says these last words in the parable: "Son, you are always with me, and all that is mine is yours. But we had to celebrate and rejoice, because this brother of yours was dead and has come to life, he was lost and has been found" (Luke 15:31–32). Fittingly, Jesus leaves unanswered the question of whether the older brother comes to the party with the joy his father enjoins. It might happen, and it might not.

Yet the parable has left us with the clear and settled impression that if the brother is to come with joy to the party, if the family is to be redeemed, then he will need to change his memory. He is going to have to come to see the past in another way than he currently sees it. The problem is, of course, that this will involve considerable disruption in the habits of seeing he has formed, those about who is his brother and his father, and even who he is himself. These habits are rooted in history. And, from what little the parable tells us, the older brother's picture of things has roots in the truth, even if not the whole truth. We can imag-

ine how he might put this: I have always been the responsible brother
. . . because of his irresponsibility, my younger brother has always been
the object of our father's worry and therefore of his focused attention
. . . our father has always been a bit soft anyway, always trying to put
the best face on a bad situation . . . and so on. How will this vision be
traded in for another, for the one his father suggests to him in his final
invitation to joy?

It may need to seep in gradually. There may be decisive times, days,
or occasions we can later look back to and say that, yes, from that day
forward everything was different. No doubt the Philippine jailer's family will tell such a story of the day the earth quaked and Paul and Silas
poured water over us. But we will not be able to notice it on the day.
Rooted as they are in time and memory, families move slowly, and redemption adapts to the pace.

Cluttered Family Memories

Redemption in families is less the stuff of brief parables or poems,
more of long and involved novels. Anne Tyler's novel *Saint Maybe* is
the story of the redemption of the Bedloe family. It begins with Danny
Bedloe's suicide after his younger brother, Ian, tells him a mixture of
truth and surmise about Danny's new wife, Lucy. Lucy had come onto
the Bedloe scene suddenly, when Danny brought her home just a few
weeks after he first met her in the post office. Tyler describes her first
appearance in the household as follows: "Here was Lucy, slender and
pretty and dressed in red, standing in the Bedloes' front hall with her
back so straight, her purse held so firmly in both hands, that she seemed
smaller than she was. She seemed childlike, in fact, although Danny
described her as a woman when he introduced her. 'Mom, Dad, Ian, I'd
like you to meet the woman who changed my life'" (3).

Ian, a high school senior, is actually attracted to Lucy: he finds her
sexy. But he is also a sharper observer than his brother, Danny, and
notices things about Lucy that suggest her stories of her past are not
entirely accurate. She already has two young children and, very shortly
after Danny and she meet, turns up pregnant with a third. When the
newborn, Daphne, arrives, it is obvious to Ian that she is not Danny's.
But Danny remains oblivious until Ian cruelly points it out—at which
point Danny drives his car full speed into a concrete wall.

Over time, the effects of Danny's death cause the Bedloe family to un-
ravel. Lucy, whose life after Danny spirals down toward dissolution, dies
of a sleeping pill overdose. Bee, Ian and Danny's mother, is heartbroken
by Danny's death and gradually gives up on life. These events only add to

Ian's already heavy weight of guilt over his brother's suicide. Ian's long redemption begins when he joins the storefront "Church of the Second Chance," where he is told by Brother Emmett, the church's leader, that to be forgiven he must offer reparation for his sin. This involves dropping out of college and raising Lucy's three children.

Haltingly, but dutifully, Ian does this. Indeed, he does it well, with the help of the Church of the Second Chance. Yet his mother's death, his father's resulting confusion and loneliness, and his own sense of his powerlessness to triumph over the snares and tensions of raising modern children—particularly Daphne, the youngest, who is most like her mother, Lucy—leave Ian's life floating and unresolved. He cannot grasp the good of his life and pin it down. He cannot return his family to its previous estate, when Danny was there and Bee presided over cheerful gatherings at Christmastime when the neighbors came for hors d'oeuvres. Nor can he carry the Bedloe family forward to some new future that completely supersedes the extended effects of his sin. As Tyler describes the state of the Bedloes late in the novel: "The family had congealed into smaller knots, wider apart, like soured milk. Their gatherings were puny, their cheers self-conscious and faint" (306).

A fresh wind must blow through the Bedloe house, one that Ian cannot himself produce. It comes in the form of Rita diCarlo: "Rita the Clutter Counselor." Rita runs her own business that specializes in cleaning houses of accumulated things—Bee's dresses, Bedloe family mementos, useless gifts from well-meaning friends—things their owners cannot bear to throw away themselves. Such clutter both embodies and symbolizes accumulated memories, a family past that once was, is now longed for, and yet cannot and will not return.

Rita turns out to be a delight for the whole family. Not only does she clean the Bedloe house, she marries Ian. Rita comes to live with Ian in the family home, where she oversees the revival of the Christmas hors d'oeuvres party for the family and the neighborhood. Further, she bears with Ian a son. In the final scene of the novel, Ian carries their newborn son downstairs into the expectant gaggle of family and friends gathered to greet the new life. As the book ends:

> [Ian] was halfway down the stairs when he felt a kind of echo effect—a memory just beyond his reach. He paused, and Danny stepped forward to present his firstborn. "Here she is!" he said. But then the moment slid sideways like a phonograph needle skipping a grove, and all at once it was Lucy he was presenting. "I'd like you to meet the woman who changed my life," he said. His face was very solemn but Lucy was smiling. "Your what?" she seemed to be saying. "Your, what was that? Oh, your life." And she tipped her head and smiled. After all, she might have said, this was an ordinary occurrence. People changed other people's lives every day of the year. There was no call to make such a fuss about it. (373)

Ian's strong memory of Lucy's arrival has heretofore been a source of pain and guilt. In this scene, the memory is not erased from his mind but rather gathered up into a new pattern. The future has remade the past so as to bear it along. Lucy's life has been taken up into a new form; it has been joined with a story whose end is not yet. It remains a sad story, but it has been joined in the many turns of Tyler's novel with a story of hope whose form could not have been the same without it. And as Tyler suggests, this is not so extraordinary. Grace and hope, we Christians believe, bear our lives up daily, including our complicated lives as families, tied, as they always are, to a past remembered and sometimes dragged along, as a great burden.

Tyler's image of memories following grooves on a phonograph record is fitting. Because family life is patterned life, these grooves are especially deep. We can get stuck in them. The patterns can even span generations, so that we do with our children what our parents did with us. The familiarity is a genuine consolation; lonely wanderers cannot know it. But for those in the groove, there is the difficulty of getting out. The answer, however, is not to stop the music altogether, but to find another groove in which the same themes can be replayed, but with other players and different endings. The story is similar, similar enough so the memory can draw out the connections, but it is not inevitably so. The sadness in one tragic story, then, is not eliminated, but rather remembered symphonically in another, perhaps in another key. No matter how much they might long for a different arrangement, however, it is not within the power of either Ian or the elder brother in Jesus's parable to write or play it. For the elder brother we never get the story; a parable is not a novel. For Ian, it comes gradually as he does his long penance for sin, learns to love, and, finally, is moved by the love of another, Rita, who arrives at the right time, cuts through the clutter, and changes the groove.

Hope for Families at the End of a Long Story

It may sound strange, but it seems to me as if the New Testament cannot spare the time to tell such long and intricate stories of grace and hope in the life of families. Instead, it opens the future into which those stories and memories can move. The older brother is offered the words of his father, but the story breaks off as Jesus conjures up new parables about how the children of light must live cunningly in the new age. Or the Philippine jailer and his whole household are saved and baptized in the space of three verses, and then are left to work this out amongst themselves as Acts carries on with the urgent story of Paul's mission throughout the whole Mediterranean world. Or Onesimus, the runaway slave, arrives home at the household of Philemon, his "owner" yet also his "brother in Christ," bearing one slim letter from the apostle Paul, the only record the New Testament gives of how family relations in a Christian slave-owning household might live into the new day.

Perhaps the New Testament did not need to spare this time precisely because its life was never meant (unless by heretics like Marcion) to be separate from the life already running through the words and stories of the Old Testament. There we have the leisure to read through the story of Joseph and his brothers, who begin their family life already weighed down by the accumulated memories of their father Jacob's preferences, including those arising from the sadness of the death of his beloved Rachel. The breach that divides this family cannot be filled in a day or a year but takes many years, and goings and comings back and forth between countries. Only then is brother Judah sufficient to the hard task of sacrificing his own good to that of his old father, Jacob, and his young brother, Benjamin, as he offers himself as a slave in Benjamin's stead to the disguised Joseph—who many years before Judah (with his other brothers) had been sold into slavery.

As scholars so often note, Joseph's story is carried along at some distance from the active God of the previous chapters of Genesis, the one who bargains with Abraham about saving Sodom or wrestles Jacob through the night. Yet we can see in Joseph's comments at the story's end the same marvel of the grace and hope Ian Bedloe feels as he bears his newborn child down the stairs. "I am your brother, Joseph, whom you sold into Egypt. And now do not be distressed, or angry with yourselves, because you sold me here; for God sent me before you to preserve life. For the famine has been in the land these two years; and there are five more years in which there will be neither plowing nor harvest. God sent me before you to preserve for you a remnant on earth, and to keep alive for you many survivors" (Gen. 45:4–7).

The message may sound trite: everything will work out in the end. But in the final paragraphs of a long family story filled up with inherited jealousies, lies, and betrayals, it takes on weight. If the hurtful family memories so many of us carry are really the last word, what are we to do? As Joseph knows, and Ian learns, we cannot by ourselves settle them. If we are to carry them forward without the "distress or reproach" Joseph here mentions, these family memories must be gathered up into a story whose ending we could have neither anticipated nor brought about: a story of grace.

Naomi Brings Ruth, and Ruth Brings Naomi

The Old Testament book of Ruth opens its narrative with a pattern that seems unbiblical: "Once upon a time," the author says, "back in the days of the judges . . ." And so we settle back for a nice little story. And Ruth is that: it is about good things that can happen in families, after terrible things have. But the steady, quiet pace of the story fits, it seems to me, the kind of grace we are offered in families. The windows are opened to the light only a little at a time. Dawn peeks in and then gradually, imperceptibly, steals over the room until we come to notice, at the end of it all, that night has become day.

Naomi, the Israelite woman whose sadness we learn of in the story's first lines, is the measure of the light. She begins truthfully by describing the blankness that has settled upon her from the outside. Her husband Elimelech is dead, and now her two sons, Mahlon and Chillion. Their Moabite widows, her daughters-in-law, Ruth and Orpah, should get on with their own lives—in Naomi's opinion. For her part, she will return alone to Israel, the homeland she and her family left to find food in Moab, where death has stalked them. There is food now in Israel, and she can live through her final days simply getting by. Otherwise, she believes she has nothing whatsoever to offer.

> Turn back, my daughters, why will you go with me? Do I still have sons in my womb that they may become your husbands? Turn back, my daughters, go your way, for I am too old to have a husband. Even if I thought there was hope for me, even if I should have a husband tonight and bear sons, would you then wait and until they were grown? Would you then refrain from marrying? No, my daughters, it has been far more bitter for me than for you, because the hand of the LORD has turned against me. (1:11–13)

Early in the story Naomi speaks this sadness with her own voice; no one else can know it. By contrast the gladness with which it is replaced by the end of the story is shared by the neighbor women, who sing as a literary chorus after Naomi receives her grandson through Ruth: "Blessed be the Lord, who has not left you this day without next-of-kin; and may his name be renowned in Israel! He shall be to you a restorer of life and a nourisher of your old age; for your daughter-in-law who loves you, who is more to you than seven sons, has borne him" (4:14–15).

It is intriguing that a book that begins and ends with Naomi's condition does not bear her name. In the title, she has given way to Ruth, who matches her in the leading role. (It is difficult to think of another biblical story that is carried so evenly by two characters.) Yet were the book named for Naomi, we might miss something: the book, which is in one sense about the state of Naomi's soul, her grief turned to joy, is more importantly about what arrives in Naomi's life. Theologically, we might name this grace. But it is grace mediated, through a person, Ruth, and through what Ruth chooses, namely the people of Israel. The oft-quoted statement made with such conviction by Ruth to Naomi, "where you go, I will go; where you lodge, I will lodge; your people shall be my people, and your God my God" (1:16), is, indeed, the springboard for all the action of the story, and therefore of Naomi's redemption. Ironically, the people of Israel reenter Naomi's life through the action of a foreigner; Ruth's act of entering a history from the outside is precisely what makes it available to Naomi from the inside.

Strikingly, Naomi refers to herself in the early part of the story as "empty" (1:21). When she first returns to Bethlehem the women (the same women who close the story with a song of joy) greet her by name. She replies: "Call me no longer Naomi, call me Mara [bitter], for the Almighty has dealt bitterly with me. I went away full, but the LORD has brought me back empty; why call me Naomi [pleasant] when the LORD has dealt harshly with me, and the Almighty has brought clamity upon me?" (1:20–21). Naomi has renamed herself in terms of her sadness—she believes she is nothing beyond it.

We might say that Naomi has been swallowed by her personal story. By "personal" I do not mean an inner story, one about her own unfulfilled dreams and aspirations, but rather a familial story that has been cut off, and, precisely because of this, seems to have become only her own. In family life she once reached out to others and with others, but her arms have been severed at the elbow. What remains is a sort of phantom pain, the kind amputees feel in their "fingers" that are no longer there. Her familial past has become, now, an absence; she can think, remember, only in terms of what once was but is no longer.

Cut off as she is, it is Naomi who needs to be embraced. This is what Ruth does. But—and this cannot be missed—Ruth's embrace is insufficient by itself to bring Naomi back. The comfort Naomi needs is not the comfort one person, even one special friend, can provide. With the death of her family, Naomi has been cut off from a future, and this cannot but make of her past a grinding and meaningless burden. There is nowhere for it to go; it simply presses down on Naomi's shoulders. By herself, Ruth may be able to shoulder some of this, but that is not what will redeem Naomi: half the weight of this burden is sufficient to crush them both. This is why the "where you go, I will go" must continue on with "your people shall be my people, and your God my God."

The great irony of Naomi's movement back home to Israel is that she cannot get there without Ruth, the foreigner from Moab. I don't mean by this she cannot find her way. Indeed, the biblical account of Naomi's arrival in Bethlehem from her journey from Moab gives us the sense that she has been walking through the desert pathways almost on autopilot. The village is astir: "Is this Naomi?" (1:19). But Naomi is glum and unresponsive: call me not Naomi but Mara, bitterness. Naomi may be back among the Israelites, but she seems to have forgotten how to be one.

At this juncture the narrative gives no further words to Naomi until after Ruth speaks. "Let me go to the field and glean among the ears of grain, behind someone in whose sight I may find favor" (2:2), she says. Here the door begins to open—not, again, by Ruth's affection directed at Naomi, but by her turn outward to the natural world and to the people who keep it. That people is Israel. Ruth, the foreigner, here takes the initiative that can bring Naomi (and Ruth with her) back into its common life. Naomi has just enough strength to consent: "Go, my daughter," she says. But Ruth is the one who goes out.

This is where the character of the people to whom Ruth reaches out makes the difference. For in Israel gleaning was a protected practice according to the Law of Moses. "When you reap your harvest in your field and forget a sheaf in the field, you shall not go back to get it; it shall be left for the alien, the orphan, and the widow, so that the LORD your God may bless you in all your undertakings. . . . Remember that you were a slave in the land of Egypt; therefore I am commanding you to do this" (Deut. 24:19–22). Will Israel remember it? An Israelite named Boaz does; he welcomes Ruth the foreign widow and allows her to glean for herself and Naomi. Boaz's faithfulness provides needed sustenance for Ruth and Naomi's bodies, but can their spirits grow?

As the story progresses, as the door opens wider to let in the light, Naomi's spirit gradually returns. She remembers the crucial provision of the Mosaic law that the next male kin must marry his deceased brother's widow. Further, it becomes clear to her that Boaz is eligible for this, since they are blood-related. So she begins to coach Ruth in the ways of personal connection. Ruth follows her advice. With each step Naomi becomes more enthusiastic for new life—and Boaz is drawn along. He claims Ruth, following Mosaic law to a T, the two marry, and Ruth bears a son, Obed, who turns out to be the grandfather of David. And, by law, Obed belongs to Naomi and Ruth. His life carries theirs forward.

Ruth and Naomi come into a new future and a new community life together. As Bret Lott works out in his quiet, sensitive novel that retells the story, Ruth and Naomi bring each other. But their life is received and carried on in the life of the people and community called Israel. In this family's case—and perhaps in any family's—accumulated memories of misfortune and sadness cannot be outlived within the life of that family alone. It needs to turns its face outward. Ruth is better equipped to do this than Naomi, and it is her courage and love that turn the tide. However, the nature of the community toward which she reaches when she resolves to look for food is equally important. The ongoing life of this family is possible only as the large political community can receive and direct her courageous initiative. Family life through time cannot redeem itself. It must be drawn up within a community whose life in time, in memory, is lived toward a wider peace. If Israel is a model, this must be a community that remembers, not just the stipulations about community life carried in its laws but the stories of trouble and struggle that lie behind them—in Israel's case, that *they* were once slaves in Egypt.

The context into which the family lives its life is essential to its redemption. The world is full of stores of rescues from family tragedy or bad luck. In the movie *Titanic*, for instance, Rose is fated to a loveless marriage with a man who cannot understand her. Jack Dawson, the third-class *Titanic* passenger of moderate artistic talent, falls in love with her, and she with him. He is her ticket to another life away from the troubles of her engagement. It is a rescue of a sort, but, fittingly, the context is a sinking ship. Such a rescue can only go on so long before it falls back upon itself. If it is to be held in the memory at all—Rose's, for she is the only one to survive—then it must be frozen into romance.

The family itself cannot be the lifeline we extend to one another for rescue from the threats of the unfriendly sea, or even from the threat of the unhappiness and boredom of family life itself. In Joseph's case, or Ruth's, or David's, the success of the redemption is due to Israel, whose laws of the land and whose ongoing story points family life beyond itself. Families who raise children only for the family, only to perpetuate its life, might as well be Mafioso, who will commit any crime to ensure the family's continued dominance.

If we return to *The Odyssey*, we can notice a paradox at its heart. The settled loyalty of the old nurse Euryclea is deep and true. She sees Odysseus as he cannot see himself, blinded as he is by his own strategic outlook formed for survival in Poseidon's territory. But Euryclea cannot match Odysseus's story for interest and adventure. In effect, we need Odysseus to leave home so we can have worthy stories to tell at our settled islands and at our tables of hospitality when he returns. The home is stationary, an isolated piece of land that humankind has managed to wrest from the wild, surrounding sea, and which it now must protect as a haven in the sea's midst.

Israel's story, however, is about a journey taken together. It is more engaging, finally, than Odysseus's, since it is not merely told and heard, but joined. Whole families can participate. The journey is based on the conviction that the whole world is the Lord's, and that he will guide his people on. Yet it also places a certain duty or responsibility upon its families as it moves them along, namely, that they remember the journey not as families only, but also as members of the people of Israel. For Israel this is the national memory as well as the memory of God's people. For Christians *nation* will likewise be a unit of memory, essential, but also sometimes seductive. In either case, family memories rise up from the body of the earth to join this bigger throng. What they join and how their memories and stories mesh will have everything to do with whether or not they can bear witness to God's redemption of the world.

Part II

Nation

4

Memory, Patriotism, and the Confession of Our Sins

From Family to Nation, on Land

The accounts of family we have considered all relate it in one way or another to land. Odysseus wanders from island to island, finally to return to his family and his homeland—even if he has trouble recognizing it. There is a famine in their homeland, so the sons of Israel leave for the land of Egypt, where later their descendents are "aliens." Naomi left the land, also for famine, but returned with the "alien" Ruth, who had become family and subsequently also great-grandmother of the great King David, who secured the national land and expanded its boundaries. Family and nation intertwine throughout the stories, always in relation to land.

The prominence of land in these ongoing stories of family and memory should not surprise. We do, after all, emerge from the soil, spring up from the ground. Earth is in one sense our mother, land our father, as the term *fatherland* suggests—or another term much in use today, *patriotism* (from the Latin *pater*, or father). We cannot omit it from our exploration of memory.

Patriotism, in fact, is based on memory, of one form or another. Moreover, like family, patriotic memories typically hold us to a place we did not choose. I am an American; I had no choice in this matter. The connection runs through the land and body.

Granted, today we have loosened these connections, due to our extraordinary mobility. This has caused some to worry that they are being pushed aside by newcomers. The worry has become a basis for nativism and exclusion: "born in the USA." In fact, the danger may run the other way. In a time when connections to land, family, and memory are loosened, or imagined as voluntary, we are prone to lie about them to ourselves, by romanticizing them. Like Odysseus on Calypso's island, we pine away for "family" and our "homeland." As with Odysseus, this is the time of our greatest temptation, for if we do not find family and nation to be just as we like, we invent them to suit us, excluding whoever does not fit our idea of ourselves. The checks on these romantic inventions—truth, humility, confession of harm done—will remain hidden from us, overwhelmed by the sentimental imaginings of our pining hearts.

Yet wherever we are, we must begin there. And the fact is that we are all in one way or another locked in connections with a family and a nation, a connection we did not make up. We may not like these connections, but if we are to remember well, we cannot ignore them.

Connection to country or nation usually follows family lines. We are members of a particular nation because our parents were. The link, again, is through body and land. It is naturally received in each of us as loyalty. By loyalty we hold fast with affection to what has been given us. Quite irrespective of their faults, we assume we should be loyal to both family and nation. Like loyalty to our own bodies, the point is not that this family or nation exceeds all other families or nations in goodness, but that it is ours. Loyalty responds to threat with defense, and sacrifice. This is one key reason why patriotic memory fixes on wars and struggles. We want to remember those who were loyal, especially loyal to death.

World War II Comes to Reading, Pennsylvania

As we have noticed throughout the Old Testament stories, perhaps especially because they are rooted in memory, families are prone to conflict. In the nation, conflict becomes war, which often is both based upon and forms memory. Almost always war relates to land. In war, families within nations spill their blood on the land for the land.

In my own family story, our relations by family to nation and war have offered a consistent challenge to my theological training, coming as that training did from two prominent American Christian pacifists, Stanley Hauerwas and John H. Yoder. My father-in-law, Robert Bolinder, achieved recognition as a fighter pilot in WWII. He flew a plane called the P-61 on night missions over sections of Western Europe as the Allies pushed Hitler's forces back toward Germany in the months following the invasion at Normandy. In the language of the U.S. Air Force, Bob had four confirmed "kills" (enemy aircraft shot down), and one suspected kill, which left him a hairsbreadth from the distinction of "flying ace" that comes with five confirmed kills.

Bob is in his eighties now. Since those few months in 1944–45 when he lost his boyhood in a daily life marked by daily death, Bob has lived his life faithfully and well. My own family and I have been graced by the gifts born of this faithfulness. As you might guess, Bob carries deeply powerful memories from this time. He has shared them often with our children and me.

Recently Bob was a speaker and honored guest at the "World War II Weekend," an aircraft show and WWII reenactment held annually on the weekend of D-day at the Reading Regional Airport in Pennsylvania. Reading is less than two hours from our home, so we drove down.

When we arrived we found that the broad space of the Reading airport was cordoned off. Forties swing music blared through the period-specific loudspeakers; WWII airplanes of every size and shape dotted the open runways; men and women and boys and girls in period dress milled through the crowd. Dumbstruck by this strange and surprising world, I drifted toward an open tent. I watched curiously as a gaggle of men in officers' uniforms posed at a table in the center of the tent. Two groups of "soldiers," one wearing the uniforms of the allies, another of the Germans (their garb and girth made me think of Sergeant Schultz on the old TV show *Hogan's Heroes*), stood solemnly by. An "officer" barked out some commands, and documents were produced. Suddenly it dawned on me that I was watching the Germans surrendering to Montgomery.

It began to rain, so I took refuge with our children under the belly of what I later learned was a B-29. Unsolicited, a man with a "volunteer guide" badge began explaining 1940s bombing technology. We gazed up at various parts in the cargo load, newly oiled and polished for our benefit, and imagined the series: switch flipped by the bombardier, hatch opened, another switch, click of the release mechanism, bomb clears the bay and floats free into the open atmosphere. Our volunteer guide offered no further insight into what came next. Once they left the cargo bay, the bombs seemed no longer to be part of his story of B-29 technology.

Meanwhile father-in-law Bob was on duty in the back of a large hangar packed with WWII enthusiasts, signing autographs at a booth next to a salvaged P-61. The P-61 is undergoing restoration—costs stand currently at roughly 1.2 million dollars. Bob's autograph on a picture of his P-61 in flight brought in ten dollars; he raised perhaps $3,000 over the weekend, a small dent in the costs. He arranged a guided tour of the restoration works, and we all stood for a family picture next to the fuselage. Three generations gathered around the pilot and his mechanical home in the skies.

As we emerged from the restricted area where the restoration was taking place, I became aware that we were breaking through a long queue that snaked through the crowded hangar: hundreds waiting patiently for something important. Bob, so it turned out, was only a minor hero that day. Paul Tibbets, pilot of the *Enola Gay*, the B-29 that dropped Little Boy over Hiroshima, Japan, was signing autographs at a table in the center of the hangar.

The WWII annual memorial in Reading is all about American loyalty and patriotic memory of a certain sort. It was also a family event, not merely for us but for most of the attendees. In the line waiting for an autograph from Paul Tibbets, fathers held babies in their arms, mothers pored over brochures with their teenagers, identifying fine points of one or the other warplane. Almost everyone was smiling and patient; the mood was festive, despite the rain. As we were transported back to the parking lot by bus, strangers offered our children the driest seats and chatted openly with them, expressing admiration when they learned of their grandfather, night-fighter pilot Bob Bolinder. I could not but appreciate their genuine kindnesses, openly extended.

And yet . . . something was missing at Reading—perhaps many things. What is being remembered? And why? What could it mean to stare up into the belly of an airplane, admiring its bombing mechanism, to shake the hand that piloted the airplane to its target over Hiroshima, gather his autograph, and go home on the bus, offering kindnesses to children along the way? In Hiroshima, if you recall, 100,000 Japanese people—mothers, fathers, brothers, and sisters, all children of God—were incinerated in the midst of their daily lives.

Going Out to See John without Seeing John

When we went to Reading, what was it we went out to see?

In Matthew 11 Jesus asks the crowd before him a similar question: When you went out to see John in the wilderness, what did you go out to see? "A reed shaken by the wind? Someone dressed in soft robes? Look, those who wear soft robes are in royal palaces. What then did you go out to see? A prophet?" "Yes," says Jesus, "more than a prophet" (vv. 7–9).

Jesus is agitated in this passage. It is one of those embarrassing ones, where he is not exactly Mr. Nice Guy. By its end Jesus tells his hearers:

"On the day of judgment it will be more tolerable for the land of Sodom than for you" (v. 24). Something has evidently gotten Jesus's goat. What is it?

Jesus is distressed at those who go out to see John in the wilderness without really seeing John in the wilderness. They go out, yes, to see, yes, to see a prophet, yes, but then everything falls in at the very center. The thing they go to see, a prophet, is turned into something else as they see him. For if John is really a prophet, one who speaks for God, then how can one go out and come back with everything still the same?

In his consternation Jesus says, "But to what will I compare this generation? It is like children sitting in the marketplaces calling to one another 'We played the flute for you, and you did not dance; we wailed, and you did not mourn'" (vv. 16–17). We dance for joy, and the flute accompanies us, and we mourn because we are sad. But Jesus's generation, and perhaps ours, has found a way around the main point. They are like children who *play* at joy and sadness, who imagine somehow that the flute or the dirge or a glimpse of the wild-eyed prophet or the B-29 or Paul Tibbets's autograph can somehow get you to the real thing, when in fact it takes you further from it.

Patriotic memory, especially when combined with the need to be loyal, has an extraordinary capacity to obscure the truth. Like those who go out to see John in the wilderness, we want to see this strange prophet. We want to feel the power of something so morally serious. This feeling, and the need for it, is sufficiently powerful in its own right to make us close our eyes on the way to see it. The feeling, the exhilaration, of having seen a real prophet blinds us so we don't take notice of what actually we have seen.

A way of describing what occurs in situations when we go out to see John, but don't see him, or when we go to Reading to remember WWII, but don't actually notice WWII, is that we turn the occasion of seeing or remembering into an *event*. I suspect this is a root of Jesus's dismay. Like the children in the marketplace, the John-watchers have turned something of utter seriousness, the word of the Lord spoken by the prophet, into something more palatable that can be contained in the memory and fed to the sentiments. "Have you seen the prophet? We have. It was amazing!"

Sentiment is the agreed-upon target of a carefully planned memory-event. Moreover, the directness with which the sentiment is pursued makes it almost an obligation. We *should* be inspired by seeing and hearing the "story" of D-day or shaking the hand of the likes of Paul Tibbets; we *should* be amazed and impressed by the extraordinary march of technological progress and the dauntless American ingenuity that brought us the victory over the Germans and Japanese; our hearts *should* be warmed by the stories told of the courage of the young men, now grown old, who faced down the enemy. As the target of the memory, sentiment also becomes its filter. We remember only those things about WWII, or we remember WWII only in such a way, as to produce the appropriate sentiment.

Fear, Death, and a Psalm

But there is more to this story of remembering WWII at Reading. My father-in-law, pilot Bob Bolinder, is also an evangelical Christian. Sentiment is quite important to evangelicals—perhaps this is their greatest liability. American patriotic sentiment runs strong through my father-in-law's heart. But there is another stream running there as well. Evangelicals, after all, are often quite serious about God, and so is Bob. This put him in a unique position among the invited speakers and pilot-heroes at the event in Reading.

Bob spoke on all three days of the event. We heard him on the second day. The crowd assembled for his talk in a large green canvas tent, authentic WWII army issue, I'm sure. Mike, a sponsor of the event and one of its designated MCs, had heard Bob's talk on the first day. He warmed us up with a bit of military humor and then introduced Bob as an "inspiring speaker" who included a "spiritual dimension" in his presentation—comments I later took to be something of a forewarning.

Bob began with some engaging stories about how he came to enlist after the shock of Pearl Harbor, what pilot training was like, and how his squadron came to fly the P-61, a new, remarkably speedy aircraft that came late to the war. At the center of his talk, however, was what he called the most important night in his life. It was December of 1944, and his squadron had been deployed in Belgium close to the German front. This was the time for what became known as the Battle of the Bulge. On this particular evening Bob's commander told his men that their orders were to stay on the ground and defend their base camp, which stood directly in the path of the German counteroffensive. These airmen had never faced combat on the ground, and most hardly knew how to fire the one small pistol they had been issued many months before. In Bob's words, "I was afraid that night, very afraid, afraid to die. But I said to myself, you claim to be a Christian—what difference is that supposed to make? So I went back to my bunk and took out my Bible. I happened to open it up to Psalm 46 where I read . . ." and here Bob asked his wife, my wife's mother, to stand up and read the whole of Psalm 46, including the following:

> The nations are in an uproar, the kingdoms totter,
>   he utters his voice, the earth melts.
> The Lord of Hosts is with us;
>   the God of Jacob is our refuge.
>
> Come, behold the works of the Lord,
>   see what desolations he has brought on the earth.
> He makes wars cease to the end of the earth;
>   he breaks the bow, and shatters the spear;
>   he burns the shields with fire.
> "Be still, and know that I am God!
>   I am exalted among the nations,
>   I am exalted in the earth." (6–10)

For a moment Bob strained the limits of the acceptable at Reading. Patriotic sentiment loses its footing in the face of these words from Psalm 46 where the kingdoms totter and God wreaks desolation on the earth. In order to regain your equilibrium you'd need to stop listening and think something like "Isn't it nice that the older woman is reading the Bible to us here in this genuine WWII army tent."

Besides reading the startling words of the psalm, Bob introduced both fear and death into the conversation. As we know, war is all about fear and death—but etiquette at a celebratory memory-event like the "World War II Weekend" keeps that unsettling thought covered up. (For instance, one does not stand for an hour in line to ask Paul Tibbets how he feels about having dropped the bomb that incinerated one hundred thousand innocent people.) In the question-and-answer session following Bob's talk, the silence returned. "Fear" and "death" were not uttered; instead questioners directed our attention back to more important topics, such as the relative advancement of radar technology in that day or the top speed of the P-61.

Patriotic memory is heavily guarded by patriotic sentiment. After all, what good is patriotism if it doesn't do something for us, doesn't inspire, doesn't bring us together? To bring us to that inspired and unified condition, there is no better means than memory, composed mainly of stories of the courage and heroism of those who, in time of crisis, protected and defended our national honor. Yet as we have been suggesting, there is a certain trouble at the heart of this configuration: needed sentiment trumps truth and turns memory into its instrument.

A question for us all, and particularly for Christians, is whether this is a *necessary* configuration. Must the memory of a people, a nation, be the instrument of patriotic sentiment? I do not think it is necessary. For in the midst of a swirl of patriotic sentiment, my father-in-law was able briefly to turn our eyes toward something more truthful. Under the conditions in Reading, this could not be sustained for much longer than five minutes. Yet we must ask what makes it possible. What sort of people do we need to be, what sort of vision do we need to have, so that we can remember well as a nation, so that we can honestly tell stories of fear and death, of tragedy, or of sin?

I think there are clues about this in the Old Testament, where we find not only the psalm Bob read the night he was so afraid, but also the stories of family we considered earlier. Imagine, for instance, what patriotic sentiment might have edited out of the story of David, whom Israel remembered as its greatest war hero. Or consider how patriotic sentiment might have changed the story of the Exodus into a brief prelude to the conquest of the Promised Land. On such a revised story, the line "you shall not oppress a resident alien; you know the heart of an alien, for you were aliens in the land of Egypt" (Exod. 23:9) might have simply disappeared and so been entirely unavailable for Ruth and Naomi.

A theme of the psalm my mother-in-law read is that God is the God of the whole earth; national purposes cannot but seem tiny and insignificant by comparison. For Israel, even though God was the God who had chosen them and promised and given them land, it was clear that God was not confined to this people and land. He was not, for God is the God of *all* creation. Hence, loyalty to Israel (or America) could not be separately defined from loyalty to this God of all. In David's story, this meant that the story of the king of Israel, God's Israel, could never simply be about who that king was *for us*, but also who he was *before this God*.

The memory of a people who tell the story in this way can open to redemption, even if it cannot bring the redemption about. If David is the king of Israel, God's Israel, then he must be accountable to God in what he does to and for this Israel, and even to and for himself and his family. So he can be both national hero and national sinner. Further, if the story of the king of Israel is told as a story of sin, Israelites who tell and remember the story are called in the telling and remembering to acknowledge their own participation in the sin with their king. National confession of sin, and the hope for redemption for a whole people, has entered the picture.

Citizenship and the Modern Nation

It may be objected that this kind of connection between, say, David and the Israelites who remembered his story as their own cannot be replicated in the modern era. Modern nations are too big and diverse. Israel was knit together by connections of blood and birth, which matter today less and less. Israel, one might say, was more like a family than a nation, as the prominence of family stories (some we have retold in earlier chapters) in its sacred text indicates. "Citizenship" in a modern nation, especially Western ones such as the United States, is often a largely bureaucratic designation, something someone can apply for and receive by paper or computer. It has little to do with memory, and surely nothing to do with corporate moral judgment and the acknowledgment of sin.

Without denying the difference, it seems to me that even modern Western nations retain sufficient traits to allow the connection. The first is *land*. While peoples can span lands—like the Kurds, or the Jews throughout most of their history—nationhood, being a "country," requires land. Not only does the land bring forth life, it also holds a past; rightly tended, it bears the marks of what once happened there. As we flit about on its surface, we may imagine that it has no power over us. Ironically, however, it remains our strongest connector.

In fact, the connectivity of the land may have increased in importance since the time of the Israelites. For instance, consider what would become of "America," an entity that currently seems so powerful, if its people were deported and sprinkled about in other lands, as Israel was, more than once. Plainly it would quickly cease to be; coherent memories of it would be unlikely to survive more than a generation. "America," in other words, is very much about land.

Established on a land, a people can emerge with a *character*, one shaped by its interaction with and history upon the land. Even if one comes to this land from elsewhere, one gets invited into this character or personality, especially as one learns its ways of acting and speaking. In America we can learn this from reading Willa Cather or John Steinbeck. These writers see how the land has grown up into the people, and they have sunk down into the land. The relation always involves a *story* by which the people of a land came to have a character.

Recently, after many years of living and working in Canada, my sister became a Canadian citizen. People at work made her a cake that said, "I am Canadian, eh?" The "eh?" says something: We Canadians are a certain way; we have a kind of corporate personality that comes out in our practices, our demeanor, our language. This is what you have become, the cake says to my sister, get used to it.

Sometimes we do, like my sister, choose our citizenship. Yet the "choice" to become a citizen is not unlike the "choice" to get married. We can control neither. When you marry someone, you suddenly become connected to a whole history or story that was not of your making, but that will, nonetheless, have everything to do with what happens henceforth. Whether you are born an American or you become one, you don't get to choose your national story. Quite despite Walt Disney and memory-events like WWII in Reading, it is not just the parts we like. As with family, if your nation happens to be screwed up, well then, you'll just have to learn to deal with it.

Citizenship involves participation with the land, character, and story of a nation. Like family, it implies moral complicity, for good or ill. Like it or not, as an American I am implicated in President Bush's invasion of Iraq. This may sound frightening, for it is a principle used by terrorists to justify killing civilians. And to be sure, it is subject to abuse. Corporate complicity requires qualification: for Christians (and most Westerners who learned it from a Christian and Jewish history), individual responsibility counts for a great deal. Jeremiah's new covenant, for instance, clearly modifies a former way of thinking that extended complicity too far: "In those days they shall no longer say; 'the parents have eaten sour grapes, and the children's teeth are set on edge.' But all shall die for their own sins" (Jer. 31: 29–30).

In the end, God will judge each of us fairly, and on our own account. And, to be sure, there are important distinctions between members of families or of nations such as the distinction between citizens and soldiers in war. Nevertheless, as we have seen, the notion of individual responsibility, infinitely extended in the other direction, toward independence and disconnection from corporate responsibility, makes us nonhumans. We become like Cyclopes. The truth lies between the extremes. And where we must begin is with the fact that we are born into community, and so born into a story already being told. While it may sometimes seem unfair to us that we inherited the communities and stories we did, I do not think we would care for the alternative, namely, to write our own story, from start to finish.

To return to David and his sins, it seems to me that when the story of the murder of Uriah (for example) is told in the Bible, the teller and the reader participate in it as they write and read it. The sin is David's, but the readers and hearers are Israelites, and they cannot but claim him. It needs to be told in its full detail as, for instance, the sins of the king of Aram or of the Philistines do not. The details matter not simply because of David, but also because of Uriah. All post-Davidic Israelites live upon his spilt blood. When Israelites tell his story with their great King David as his murderer, they participate in it—they confess, in a way, that they are responsible for his death.

Acknowledgment of such implications and complicities is not easy. As was evident in Reading, if we could choose, we would rather talk of bombs before they drop or about pilots in their speeding airplanes rather than alone in their bunks fearing death. This preference, coupled with the need to build up our patriotic sentiment, leads to patriotic memory that bends the truth and closes itself to the confession of sin.

In the current time, we seem caught between two contradictory tendencies. For so long as we see ourselves as individuals separate from communities, our natural tendency is to *observe* what goes on in these communities rather than to participate in them. Yet this deception, that we are observers and not participants, seems also to hide from us the responsibility we have to tell the story truthfully, and so we give in to our sentimental desires to make the story into whatever we'd like it to be. The movement in one direction seems to carom back in the other. Precisely because we are individuals who feel disconnected from family and nation, when we feel suddenly the force of our connection, we want the story to give us what we need to feel proud to be a part of it. And so we edit out the troubled parts, the fear and death, the suffering and the sin.

Opening the Hidden Wound

There must be space in national memory for us to be reminded of the personal linkages that connect us to what others have suffered. These linkages are everywhere. For instance, I referred earlier to the awakening of my own family memory on a trip to the summer cottage I love so well. However, it is a fact that, while an extremely honest and principled one, my father was a corporate businessman—that was the origin of the money he used to buy the summer cottage we all loved so well. Recently we had friends from Uganda in East Africa stay with us in our home. In passing I referred to our vacation at our "summer cottage." They did not know the phrase. Their incomprehension brought me face to face with the fact that I belonged to a people for whom the possession of a "summer cottage" or "second home" was nothing out of the ordinary.

In an extraordinary book called *The Hidden Wound*, Wendell Berry sets about to explore the painful linkages that tie him by family and tradition to the American institution of slavery. White southerners, Berry's family participated invariably and inevitably in a way of life that carried—and still carries—the effects of slavery and the racism that supported it. Berry knows he is implicated in this history. But the specifics need telling.

Berry's great-grandfather, John Johnson Berry, owned slaves. Family stories indicate he was a gentle and mild man who, by the going standard, treated his slaves well. However, as Berry notes, "in spite of the self-defensive myth of benevolence, it was impossible for the slave owner to secure any limit to the depth or the extent of his complicity: as soon as he found it necessary to deal with the slave as property he was in as deep as he could go" (7).

The complicity is revealed by a story Berry tells, also passed down in family lore. "John Johnson Berry once owned a slave who was a 'mean nigger,' too defiant and rebellious to do anything with."

As Berry notes, speaking or even knowing such inherently violent language marks us. But, as the story continues, John Berry lacked the temperament and will to do anything with this man, so he sold him to a local slave buyer by the name of Bart Jenkins. "Having completed his purchase, Bart Jenkins came in the night, and knocked the man on the head while he was asleep, and bound him, and led him away with a rope" (7).

While they did nothing to stop him, almost certainly Berry's ancestors were shocked by Bart Jenkins's act. Other stories of the man survive in Berry family lore, each tinged with distaste. The stories match a characterization of Jenkins given in a romanticized account of the "Kentucky Cavaliers" by George Dallas Mosgrove, written at the end of the nineteenth century, wherein Mosgrove turns Jenkins's angry and violent spirit into glory. "He was a stalworth knight and keen—And had in many a battle been—His eyebrow dark and eye of fire—showed spirit proud and prompt to ire . . ." (19).

Berry's exemplary work in *The Hidden Wound* is to find his own complicity as a Berry and as a white American in the violence visited on so many African Americans in slavery. He finds the double violence inside Mosgrove's stories, first of the man to whom his great-grandfather once sold a slave, and, second, of the romanticized account of him as a southern hero. As Berry reports more words from Mosgrove: "Captain Bart Jenkins and a number of other officers were asleep in Abingdon when the Federals entered town. Captain Jenkins was captured successively by two soldiers. He killed both of them and escaped from the town" (12).

The title of Berry's book turns our eyes in the right direction: "the hidden wound." Here is how he describes it:

> If the white man has inflicted the wound of racism upon the black man, the cost has been that he would receive the mirror image of that wound into himself. As the master, or as a member of the dominant race, he has felt little compulsion to acknowledge it or speak of it: the more painful it has grown the more deeply he has hidden it from himself . . .
>
> This wound is in me, as complex and deep in my flesh as blood and nerves. I have borne it all my life, with varying degrees of consciousness, but always carefully, always with the most delicate consideration for the pain I would feel if I were somehow forced to acknowledge it. . . . [Yet now] I want to know, as fully and exactly as I can, what the wound is and how much I am suffering from it. And I want to be cured; I want to be free from the wound myself, and I do not want to pass it on to my children. (4)

Berry knows that this last line about not passing the wound on to his children may overreach. In fact, he knows this especially well, since the stories he tells subsequently in the book, with words like "mean nigger," were carried on in his family without any clear intent. He knows he also may pass on the wound in some newly hidden way. However, these limits to our control do not excuse us from looking as closely as we can upon what we have received from the past, and how we received it.

The task of remembering and even confessing a hidden national wound of the sort racism and slavery are for America does not completely remove it. Indeed, the sort of entity that America is, a nation among nations, limits what effect memory as confession can have. A nation is not the church, the only community I know of whose life is built (or is supposed to be built) on the confession and forgiveness of its sins. The confession that is a fixture in the liturgy: "We confess that we have sinned against you in thought, word and deed . . ." is not transferable to the nation (or even the family) since participation in either one is not based on the confession and the forgiveness. Put another way, family and nation are "natural communities" as the church is not: we are born into family and nation, but not into church. And we join the latter only as we confess and are forgiven of our sins.

Nevertheless, the kind of confession offered in Berry's book has its own unique character with unique effects. These differ from, for instance, the confessions of Augustine. Augustine tells of his individual sins in detail—his resistance to his teachers, how he stole from a pear tree, his addiction to sex, etc. We think of these as things the individual Augustine decided to do that he shouldn't have. By contrast, Berry's "confession" in *The Hidden Wound* is not about his choice but about his *participation* in sin by *inheritance*. The inheritance came to him most directly by family, but—and here is an important factor—Berry's family was no different from any other white family similarly situated in America. This changes how we receive his story morally. Upon reading Augustine we say, you know, I remember doing something like that when I was younger. Upon reading Berry, we say, I do not know it very well, but as a white American I am sure my family history also connects me to this national racist history. In the latter case, the sins we become aware of are not mine but *ours*.

It may be said again that we can overextend complicity. After all, isn't it Berry (and perhaps Pinches) as white males who need to confess racism? To imply that African Americans similarly participate may seem pernicious. And what about recent American immigrants whose family history had no touch whatsoever with slavery in America? To be sure, it is true that either by their own direct activity, inherited role, or family lineage, some Americans are more closely connected to the sins of slavery, or the sins of WWII such as Hiroshima, or the ongoing sins of ecological destruction. Moreover, there will be Americans whose connection by activity, role, or family to such sins is principally on the other side, so to speak, as victims rather than as perpetrators: African Americans, Native Americans, Japanese Americans, etc.

But here is where Berry's term *wound* helps especially. Racism is, Berry says, a wound inflicted by the white man in the black man, and its cost is "the mirror image of that wound" that the white man takes "into himself." As a white man, Berry undoubtedly has a different set of responsibilities as he tells the story of this wound, as he brings it into his own life, than does the grandson or granddaughter of the slave his family sold to Captain Jenkins. Both, however, must tell this story, carry it with them in their memories, and pass it to their children. Their responsibilities in the telling will be different; for instance, perhaps the slave's grandchild will need to learn to remember and not resent, as Berry will need to remember and confess. But both Americans—indeed all Americans—will need to remember well and truthfully what was done and suffered.

Sin and Confession

Yet the language of sin cannot be dispensed with entirely. *Wound*, after all, can be turned in another way: toward victim and victimizer. Berry's wound is reciprocal, and carried in different ways by black and white Americans together. As such, all Americans have some part in it, complicity of one or the other sort. We might, however, escape this by pointing fingers. Our own current culture is becoming adept at this, with blame becoming a key operative term.

The language of sin and confession will not allow this, especially if we add in St. Paul's point that "all have sinned and fall short of the glory of God" (Rom. 3:23). Yet theologically it will take careful work to sustain the language, especially at this national level. Unlike Israel in the Bible, America does not have its own God. Israelites had a place not only for their confession but also for the absolution of their sins, namely, the temple in Jerusalem. But the temple is no more—Christian Americans, in fact, have a stake in not rebuilding it in such a place as Washington, D.C., for they believe the temple moves, now, throughout the world in the "place" called church. This is why, *contra* the likes of Pat Robertson, it is a mistake for Christians to "restore" the "Christian God" to America.

Confession begun at a national level may need to move elsewhere to find its completion. The first step, though, can occur there, namely, detailing, with a sense of participation and complicity, those parts of the American (or Canadian, or Ugandan, etc.) history that were especially brutal and sinful. Confession of sin will need to make its way finally to a particular god, or so I believe, but it seems that it might—in fact it can and must—begin within the corporate story of a nation. At the beginning it is perhaps sufficient to establish the truthful story of what once was done here, in our name, on this soil, for this nation. Put another way, as Americans we can together remember our sins, even if we cannot together receive forgiveness and absolution.

An essential task for Christian Americans is to name and remember the sins of America as they recognize them as Christians. This may sometimes test the range of the acceptable in public discourse, as I believe Bob Bolinder did in Reading. Importantly, however, the exercise of remembering and retelling both in his case and in Wendell Berry's is not just national but personal. Since citizenship implies both participation and complicity, it cannot exclude the connection between the personal and national in particular citizens, nor can it predetermine its form. We can continue to hope that this implication of "shared citizenship" is sufficient to allow truthful national memory a common space in which to grow.

5

National Memory at Gettysburg

Remembering at the Site of Your Choice

I don't know how the annual World War II memory-fest came to be held in Reading, Pennsylvania, although the story, I'd guess, has something to do with money: someone had some, was ready to part with it under certain conditions, and happened to care about Reading. Otherwise, the *location* of Reading has nothing whatsoever to do with WWII, at least nothing more than any other American town from which soldiers came to fight and die in WWII. Among other things, this means that the site of the memory-fest, the Reading airport, needed to be made into something it never was for the sake of the memory.

I believe this is part of the temptation of the national "remembering" that goes on annually at Reading. Since we begin with the land as a blank slate, we can make it into whatever we like, indulging our romantic fancy. Music over crackling loudspeakers sets the mood . . . some of us dress up, as if going to the prom . . . we bring in some war heroes of the past, the kind they just don't make anymore. This is how we transform Reading, PA, for the weekend to be just like how we think it was wherever it was that WWII took place. And afterward, we all head back to work on Monday morning.

I do not mean to say it is wrong to remember World War II in Reading. If they are to remember WWII, Americans must do it someplace. Short of flying to France, which most of them cannot do, Americans must remember WWII where it did not occur—so why not in Reading? This is what comes of modern warfare technology and "superpower" status: the blood nations spill soaks into soil that has otherwise no place in national memory. So it remains largely inaccessible to those among the living who remain connected, by family and citizenship, to the spilt blood. Nevertheless, it is the task of these living ones to remember. We must be careful, then, not to blame Americans overmuch for spectacles like Reading.

That said, the absence of the self-same soil on which the blood was spilt opens to a key abuse in national memory with respect to war. If you stand on the soil where the blood once ran you cannot avoid the annoying truth that on this very same soil once flowed the blood of the enemy. This is a truth that seemed absent in Reading.

Coming to Gettysburg

About eighty miles southwest from Reading lies another town in Pennsylvania where this truth is not so easily avoided: Gettysburg. Here was fought the most important and bloodiest battle of the American Civil War.

Gettysburg's location is in one sense an accident: there was no Union stronghold here that Confederate forces came to attack; it was just a little town where the roads crossed. Wanting to move the war from his native Virginia, where it had come to put considerable stress on the land and its people, General Robert E. Lee took his Army of Northern Virginia north along the Shenandoah Valley, through Maryland and into Pennsylvania where it became the Cumberland Valley, and then began to curl southeast. His hope was to draw Union troops up from their capital for an engagement in the open, which, if it could be won, might shatter the Union army and leave a path open to Washington. That engagement happened to occur at Gettysburg.

In another sense, however, the location of the decisive battle at Gettysburg was far from accidental. Arguably, the land at Gettysburg won the battle. Unlike at Reading or with WWII, if you are an interested American citizen, you can go see this land, climb its hills, walk its fields, and remember.

I have done this more than once. During my last visit I traced along the High Water Mark Trail that winds south from Cemetery Hill, where President Lincoln delivered his famous address. This hill is now the hub of the national military park that covers the area of this most famous Civil War battle. The house that was once the headquarters of General George G.

Meade, the commander of the Army of the Potomac, is on the trail. The trail bears its name because of the historical claim that the third and final day of battle marked the high point of the power of the Confederacy—the high water mark. On that day, July 3, 1863, twelve thousand Rebel soldiers charged across the broad and open expanse separating Seminary Ridge, from which they had traded cannon fire with the Unionists for two days, and Cemetery Ridge, where the Union soldiers were well dug in, waiting for the Confederate attack.

The day I visited was warm, but not so warm as the sweltering heat of those three awful days of July 1863. I had come in September, and children were back in school. The grassy area around the "copse of trees"—where the Confederate soldiers aimed their attack—was swimming with young students on school field trips. Guides in Union dress, obviously well trained to handle the confusion, were leading them about. I stopped to watch one planned exercise. A guide had assigned the children letters: the "A" group, the "B" group, the "C's" and so on. Once lettered, they began in a cluster on the lower side of a gradual grassy rise and ran east, right over the last few yards of ground George Pickett's forces once covered under the steady rain of deadly Union fire. As the children ran the guide called out: "A's drop," then "B's drop," "C's drop," and so on until only a small number of the children remained standing at the end of the charge. The dead and wounded children were soon gathered with the living and herded back on the bus—off to do some more "remembering," perhaps in the Cyclorama Center, where is housed the famous painting in the round by Paul Philippoteaux of Pickett's Charge, the same event the children were reenacting.

Almost everyone has heard of Pickett's Charge. Its power in American national memory shows us something of its selectivity. Pettigrew also charged, and Trimble, but we remember them less. Pickett, in fact, owes a good deal of his notoriety to Philippoteaux's painting, which, after years touring the nation's cities, came to the park in 1941 and since has been housed in a curious round structure that visitors feel obliged to stop and see. The extraordinarily popular historical novel *The Killer Angels*, by Michael Shaara (1974), also accents Pickett, as well as, on the Union side, Col. J. Lawrence Chamberlain, the commander of the Twentieth Maine, a division that helped hold Little Round Top on the second day of the battle and also participated in the fight against Pickett and company on the third. The movie *Gettysburg* (1993) is a good deal based on *The Killer Angels*, and both Pickett and Chamberlain are portrayed by stars; Chamberlain's character, in fact, could be thought to carry the leading role of that movie. A guide I hired on one of my visits complained that people often arrive with the impression that the Twentieth Maine won the battle for the Unionists.

Impressions, or little bits of knowledge, swirl around a place like Gettysburg, where thousands come to participate in some way in the exercise of nationally remembering. As I made my way back from the "copse of trees" toward the cyclorama parking lot, I stopped at the base of the majestic statue of Gen. George Meade on his horse. A father was expressing some surprise to his daughter that Meade had been so honored, since, after all, he had subsequently been relieved of his command by Lincoln. The president was disappointed by Meade's lack of resolve in pursuit of Lee as he retreated south after Gettysburg. This was true, but it is also true that Meade did an extraordinary job at Gettysburg, especially given that he had received his command over the Army of the Potomac just three days before the battle began. Like Meade, we all have very little control over which parts of our lives we will be remembered for.

The matter of whether Meade should be honored for his service with such a monument is something that can be cleared up fairly easily by investigation, which this father had not yet done. With Gen. Robert E. Lee, the considerations are somewhat different. Since Gettysburg was the one major battlefield north of the Mason-Dixon Line, it could not but become a center for post–Civil War Union pride. In the decades directly following the conflict, northern partisans, many of them veterans of the battle, erected most of the thousands of smaller markers and monuments that dot the battlefield. Yet time wore on and official concern to unify the nation opened to the suggestion that southern states might also want to erect monuments in honor of their heroes and fallen ones. So it was that the State of Virginia drew up a plan for an impressive monument on the ground of Seminary Ridge that would feature General Lee on his horse, Traveler. In 1903 Civil War veterans in Philadelphia got wind of the plan and were scandalized. Here are the words of a resolution they passed in protest.

> What Gettysburg is we and our comrades have made it. The glory, the fame, the sentiment that cluster around the very name of Gettysburg . . . is all ours and to the memory of our fallen comrades. . . . [W]e appeal to the Senators and Representatives in the legislature of our state to defeat this insult to the memory of our dead defenders . . . who gave their energies and the best efforts of their youth to overthrow the man whose statue it is proposed to place in honor upon the soil he desecrated and which the blood of our comrades made sacred. (Platt, 30)

It does little good to complain about views expressed by the ill-informed father or these passionate veterans. Corporate memories such as those carried by a nation will be of necessity selective and partisan—just as they are in Reading. Yet this is where Gettysburg holds its place. As opposed to the surreal venue of Reading, the *place* Gettysburg affords a real venue in which these selective stories and contested understandings can continue to be told and investigated. The place does not settle the disputes, but it holds them to its ground. If you want to remember, you have to get out and let your feet touch this ground the veterans call sacred.

Sacrifice on the Wheat Field

A place less traveled over by visitors' feet than the High Water Mark Trail is to be found to its south, midway between the rocky ground of "Devil's Den" and the peach orchard into which Gen. Daniel Sickles moved his Union troops in the second day of the battle. Sickles judged, without Meade's approval, that it could be better defended against an attack of the Confederates. His move strung out the Union troops at the base, or southern end, of the "fishhook" formation into which Meade had arrayed his troops, following the topography of Cemetery Ridge. The ridge gained the Union forces a broad yet defensible stand on the high ground from which to receive and hopefully stave off the Confederate onslaught.

On that day, July 2, Lee had decided to send two wings of attack against the Union positions, one at the north and eastern end of the Union line—at Culp's Hill—and one at its southern end, in the region of the Round Top hills, Big and Little. Gen. James Longstreet, the commander of the southern Confederate flank, spent most of the day marching his troops south along Seminary Ridge so as to avoid detection and bombardment from Union cannon. In the late afternoon, Longstreet finally was able to cross the broad fields separating the two ridges and throw his men into the strange mixture of geography that happened to mark the southern end of the Union line. The ground of Devil's Den and Little Round Top, today as then, is broken by rock outcroppings and strewn over by huge granite boulders. Longstreet's attack was powerful, and Union forces were unable to hold out for long. Devil's Den fell to the Confederates by 4:00 p.m., and they soon began to advance northward, hoping to penetrate the Union defenses, gain the high ground, and encircle the Union troops, eventually joining with the Confederate left flank attacking under the command of Gen. A. P. Hill.

As Longstreet's men advanced northward against Sickle's strung-out defenses, they came upon a nineteen-acre plot of ground planted in wheat by Gettysburg farmer George Rose. Union troops had set up on a stone wall at the southern end of the field under the cover of battery firing "canister," cannon shells packed with small shot and sawdust designed for close-in fighting. These exploded like a modern shotgun shell and sprayed their deadly projectiles at charging human bodies. To the Rebels' advantage, however, woods ringed the wheatfield and provided good cover for the advancing attack.

These factors combined to make the wheatfield a whirlpool of death and destruction. The fighting raged over its ground for more than three bloody hours, until darkness began mercifully to cloak flags and faces, making killing more difficult. Throughout the battle in the wheatfield, reinforcements for both sides arrived at intervals, giving a pattern of thrust and counterthrust. The field changed hands some six times. Blue and gray moved back and forth through the stalks of grain, planted with the hope of harvest and sustenance, but on this most horrible day trampled to the earth, mixed in with so much blood. It was said by observers at the end of day that in parts of the field one might altogether avoid touching the earth as one walked, stepping rather from body to body. Some four thousand men, dead or wounded, covered the field. Brigades such as the Sixty-first New York or the Fifty-third Pennsylvania lost close to 60 percent of their number. Confederate brigades also typically lost at least one-third of their men.

July 2, 1863, is now more than 140 years past. If one goes to the wheatfield today and walks over its ground, one finds that it lies in an uneasy peace. The land is sprinkled with monuments, some marking where a commander fell, or where a brigade held fast. The words chiseled in stone are affectionate, full of praise and remembered details of that day. Someone very much hoped that we would not forget what happened on the wheatfield on July 2, 1863.

Lincoln Goes Out to See Gettysburg

Suppose we consider once again Jesus's question: When you went out to see John in the wilderness, what did you go out to see?—a reed shaken by the wind? When we go to Gettysburg, when we walk the wheatfield, what is it we are hoping to see?

At the Gettysburg Chamber of Commerce, they will count my visits or those of the schoolchildren on buses as "tourism." But it seems a misnomer. It is easier to be a tourist at Reading than at Gettysburg—easier still at, say, Disney World, where a whole world has been designed for your pleasure. What is a better description? We go to Gettysburg not as tourists but to remember. And the difference is, remembering is not about we who remember, but about the thing remembered. Those who went out to see John in the wilderness, the ones who so unnerved Jesus, were first-century tourists. Their seeing John was not really about John at all, but about them, the tourists.

This is not to imply by contrast that rememberers are obliterated or lost in the remembering. Rather, in the remembering they become *participants* in the thing remembered. Remembering that goes on at Gettysburg is, it seems to me, necessarily participatory, particularly for the citizens of the very same nation into whose history the battle of Gettysburg fits. So the difference between tourism and remembering lies in the participation. Tourists come to see, rememberers come to share.

For Americans, there is a prototype for "going to Gettysburg" laced into the story of Gettysburg itself: Abraham Lincoln's visit in November of 1863. In his famous address on the occasion of that visit, Lincoln turns quickly to this matter of why we come. We come to participate in an action that marks the ground: "to dedicate a portion of that field, as a final resting place for those who here gave their lives." But, as Lincoln goes on, any power in these acts of dedication is dependent on the far greater power of the soldiers who fought the battle. "But, in a larger sense we cannot dedicate—we cannot consecrate—we cannot hallow—this ground. The brave men, living and dead, who struggled here, have consecrated it, far above our poor power to add or detract. The world will little note, nor long remember what we say here, but it can never forget what they did here."

This last line, one of the best known in the address (after, of course, "four score and seven years ago"), is somewhat ironic, since its claims have turned out false, at least with "remembering" and "forgetting" understood in a certain sense. Surely the address is more widely "remembered"—more frequently rehearsed and recited—than the battle. (The other day I heard a parody of the address as the main text of a television commercial for an appliance superstore.) Yet if we take Lincoln to mean remembering as an activity of participation that links the remembered with what went before, then we can accept the point. What happened on Rose's wheatfield on July 2, 1863, is the thing, and Lincoln's address and visit, and all subsequent visits, draw out their meanings in terms of it.

When we go out to the wheatfield as rememberers, we go to participate, to join ourselves and our lives in some sense with the monumental thing that occurred there. This is not simply an act of emotion, although it may be emotional. Rather, once joined, the story can no longer be a good and heroic story or even a horrible and tragic story. For Americans who come to remember at Gettysburg, it is *our* story—our extraordinary, heroic, horrible, and tragic story.

In a moment I shall also want to limit this participation, especially for Christians. But I do not want to miss here what the wheatfield tells us. Human memory, as we have noted in previous chapters on family, is a bodily thing. Not only is it drawn out in us by bodily memories—smells and sounds—but it springs, as we do, from the earth. The power of memory derives not from what was chosen but from what was given. Humanly, this stands as a sign to us that we are more gift than accomplishment, more what we were made to be by others than what we have made of ourselves.

But what is the nature of the gift? In the first order, it is of sustenance, nourishment, strength of body and mind. We receive these from our mothers and fathers, as they received it from theirs. The linkage of family through time is in this sense a line of life and growth. Yet perhaps on the pattern of the first story in Genesis, wrapped tightly together with this story of life and growth is also one of enmity, destruction, and death. Things go terribly wrong—some of the "gifts" we receive from the past are of a much darker sort. Rightly, memory grips with equal force the bad and the good. In Gettysburg, at the wheatfield, what was planted and tilled with care for life's enrichment was cut off and trampled in death. Men's bodies, grown strong on the sustenance of food and family, in North and in South, were cut down and mingled into the soil with the life-giving wheat. The land at Gettysburg received them both.

But of course the land does not remember—we who spring from it do. And so we mark the land, "consecrate" it, as Lincoln would have it, in relation to what happened to us there. This, it seems to me, is one of the key functions of national memory: it marks the land in relation to us and so marks us in relation to the land. Participation in national memory is acknowledgment of how we are so marked in our joys and sorrows, lives and deaths. It expands and fills out family memory in relation to place by acknowledging that this marking is more than biological or genetic but human and communal. Through nation my link with those who killed and perished on the wheatfield, while less strong than with my father, is nevertheless real and present. My life and death cannot but be lived out in some sort of relation to the life and death of the nation, and to those who on the wheatfield contested its past and future.

What we must see, however, with national memory more so than familial, is that the nation will want to put this connection and participation that comes with memory to work for its own end. Unlike families, nations profess "purposes." This is especially true of modern nation-states with expansive borders and millions of citizens. In a local community it is easier to see what we share simply as daily living. My neighborhood, for instance, does not really have a corporate purpose: we simply live together. Of course the nation-state's purpose can be related to this simply living: its task is to allow for it, sometimes protecting its conditions. Nevertheless, as soon as we have an entity whose self-description is purpose-driven, then it will look for ways to uphold and further these purposes, whatever they may be.

Lincoln does this in his address with memory: "The world will little note, nor long remember what we say here, but it can never forget what they did here." Next sentence: "It is for us the living, rather, to be dedicated here to the unfinished work which they who fought here have thus far so nobly advanced. It is rather for us to be here dedicated to the great task remaining before us—that from these honored dead we take increased devotion to that cause for which they gave the last full measure of devotion"—on to the famous last line—"we here highly resolve that these dead shall not have died in vain—that this nation, under God, shall have a new birth of freedom—and that government of the people, by the people, for the people, shall not perish from the earth."

Obviously these are inspiring words. Yet their effects could be chilling. Once the "last full measure of devotion" has been given by some of its sons and daughters, national memory is not generally very well equipped to ask if the unfinished work for which they gave it should be continued.

In Lincoln's case, one can perhaps excuse how the words work, drawing the memory of the dead soldiers' cause up into the causes of the living. There was justice in the cause, and it needed to be carried forward. Yet the move had one clear effect: it separated the dead on the wheatfield. For there were opposing causes, and only half died for the one Lincoln championed.

Lincoln's Latter Words

Today you can find Lincoln seated at the end of the long open ground and past the simple rectangular shape of the reflecting pool that extends the National Mall westward, in Washington, D.C. Lincoln sits stone-faced in his memorial or "shrine," like a judge, gazing impassively out over the national confusion.

Whenever I walk this broad expanse, from the free-standing obelisk by which we remember George Washington, to the foot of the steps of Lincoln's shrine, I cannot help but think of Richard John Neuhaus's phrase "the naked public square," particularly because this is the place where we passionately place one cause and then another before the nation on the weekends, only to return to our daily routines on Monday morning. What Neuhaus means by his term is that in the current climate of modern politics, public discourse has been emptied of significant content, individualized or therapized into the language of "our rights," so as to obscure from us the common goods, often rooted in religious traditions, that are genuinely worth contesting in a republic. The empty ground of this Mall contrasts significantly with the ground at Gettysburg, which is so generously peppered with markers and monuments, big and little.

I do not mean this necessarily as a criticism: there is significance in open space. Moreover, something I saw when I last walked this span could not have occurred had there been a marker. A group of boys in blue blazers, preppies in about the ninth grade, were walking up the steps of the Lincoln Memorial. One of them was black, the others white. The black youth stopped at a point on the steps and said excitedly: "This is where he stood!" Some of his companions did not know to what he referred, so he had to tell them. He was referring, of course, to Martin Luther King Jr.'s delivery of his "I Have a Dream" speech before the crowds who had marched on Washington for the civil rights of African Americans. That march occurred, rather ironically, almost one hundred years to the day after those who died on the wheatfield at Gettysburg gave the "last measure of devotion." That this boy had the opportunity to testify to his classmates about this event seemed important to me. They had to listen to him rather than simply run their eyes over some words on a stone marker.

It is words, spoken or written, that guide our memories. Blood and soil awaken them. But, for good or ill, words direct national memory, toward either truth or delusion. When I visit the Lincoln Memorial, I find that I am forever grateful to the person or committee who made the decision that not only the entire Gettysburg address but also the second inaugural address should be chiseled in the flat marble surrounding the silent statue.

The second inaugural address begins in a businesslike manner. You know as much as I do, says Lincoln, that the Civil War, which has dragged out for almost two years since Gettysburg, is the nation's main concern. We shall all simply have to wait to see how and when it ends. "With high hope for the future, no prediction in regard to it is ventured."

And so Lincoln passes to a seemingly dispassionate description of the conditions that gave rise to the war. He concludes the discussion in this way: "Both parties deprecated war; but one of them would make war rather than let the nation survive; and the other would accept war rather than let it perish. And the war came."

One might worry that this last sentence is too passive to be uttered by a wartime president. Presidents, after all, declare wars and wage them; they do not simply receive and endure them. Yet Lincoln's description reminds us that wars often arise out of bad histories; they are products of the dark gifts, better called curses, that have passed between generations of families and citizens, borne along in the steam of story and memory that families and nations keep. Whatever one might want to say to Lincoln about what he could have done as president to avoid the war, one cannot deny the presence at the heart of the war of a very bad history: the specter of slavery.

The tone of the second inaugural address changes at roughly mid-point, where it takes a strong turn toward theology. One might think this comes when Lincoln marks that the two sides that had come to be at war "read the same Bible, and pray to the same God." Yet this is a gesture toward the Bible, rather than a look within it, which is where Lincoln is headed. While absent from the first half of the address, the second half is laced through with quotations from scripture. These begin with Matthew 7:1 (KJV): "judge not that ye be not judged." But Lincoln moves quickly beyond this to a more obscure quote from Jesus in Matthew: "Woe unto the world because of offences! For it must needs be that offences come; but woe to that man by whom the offence cometh!" (Matt. 18:7 KJV).

For Lincoln in 1865 woe was clearly upon the nation, and it had come of offense. In the passage, however, Jesus is interested not just in the woe and the offense, but in the one from whom the offense came—and Lincoln sees this. Here he might have turned and assigned blame to what was then the other side: the Rebels are the offenders, and it is they who have brought the woe upon us all. Many factors keep him from this. Politically, he wants to unify and not divide. Furthermore, it is true that unlike any other war in American history, this one literally pitted friend against friend, father against son, and brother against brother. But deeper, perhaps, for Lincoln is a theological sense of our joint and corporate participation in sin. As woe, supposes Lincoln, God "gives to both North and South this terrible war." We rightly hope and pray the scourge will soon pass. "Yet, if God wills that it continue until all the wealth piled by the bond-man's two hundred and fifty years of unrequited toil shall be sunk, and until every drop of blood drawn by the lash, shall be paid by another drawn with the sword, as was said three thousand years ago, so still it must be said, 'The judgments of the Lord, are true and righteous altogether.'"

One practical effect of these theological words is that the blood spilled on the wheatfield does not need to be typed. All of it is, in effect, atoning blood. The nation has committed sins, many, no doubt, but one in particular, here clearly named. And so the nation is receiving its punishment, from the hand of the one true and righteous judge of all.

The rousing end to the Gettysburg address is replaced in this later, deeper document by another sort of work. The memory of the sacrifice of those who gave the "last measure of devotion," what Lincoln used at Gettysburg in hopes that he might inspire "a new birth of freedom," seems to have been humbled. And so we come to the last, long, and extraordinary sentence of the address:

> With malice toward none; with charity for all; with firmness in the right, as God gives us to see the right, let us strive on to finish the work we are

in; to bind up the nation's wounds; to care for him who shall have borne the battle, and for his widow, and his orphan—to do all which may achieve and cherish a just, and a lasting peace, among ourselves, and with all nations.

These are not the words of a fighter. Perhaps Lincoln had little fight left in March of 1865, just a few weeks before his death by assassination. But they seem to me to be truer words to place over the wheatfield at Gettysburg, and other wheatfields the earth over where nations have clashed and men's blood has been spilt. We go on after such clashes and carry the memory of them with us, but the work the memory opens to us is not so much about vindicating or redoubling noble efforts as it is about gathering what remains of life, nourishing and cherishing it.

Yet such a judgment may depend upon the understanding that holds so firmly in the final paragraphs of Lincoln's second inaugural address, namely, that the nations are subject to the true and righteous Judge. National memory outside of such a judgment seems prone to gather and billow, like angry clouds before a storm. Like family memory, while it seems often to reach out for redemption, even to intuit its need for it, national memory does not contain within itself its own salvation. Such an extraordinary force it is, but it waits for direction from the winds of spirit and word. We cannot tell which way the winds shall blow.

Confession, Sacrifice, and the Soil

Going to Gettysburg will not by itself ensure remembrance; conversely, one might go to Reading and remember well. Nevertheless, conditions on the ground make a difference. What are the differences in the conditions? It is not at all as if the "mood" is better set in Gettysburg, or that Reading lacked "authenticity." In fact, in Reading you could grasp the real and living fingers that brought Little Boy down on the real heads of one hundred thousand Japanese. There is nothing like that in Gettysburg.

What is lacking in Reading but present in Gettysburg is what Lincoln calls the "consecrated ground." As he saw, words by themselves are powerless to hallow the earth. We need blood—death, really.

One can see this at roadsides throughout America. Here at a curve, beside a tree, is a wreath staked in the ground or plastic flowers secured to a cross. We wonder as we drive by these little roadside shrines how it is that a parent or loved one could stand to come back. Wouldn't this be the last place you'd want to come—where the precious body of your son or daughter, husband or wife, had been gashed and broken in an automobile wreck, their life ebbing away under the weight of mangled steel? Something powerful and mysterious must draw these ones back; they want to touch the earth where the life of their loved one ran out.

You can go to Reading, reminisce about war, and avoid death. This you cannot do at Gettysburg. It is all around, sunk in the soil over which your living feet pass. Death, as we have often heard, is the great equalizer. When you walk the ground at Gettysburg, you cannot but think: this is where a man died, many men. And this leads to the next thought: he was a man like me! Surely he knew something of the goodness of life and so also of the deep, gnawing fear of death.

The touch of the hallowed ground has the extraordinary power to bring us suddenly contemporaneous with those who went before, those who died upon it. So we ask ourselves: Who was this man, the young man who died here, and what was he thinking as he died? Did he call out for God? For his mother? And when it came, how did she take the news?

These are individualized questions that surround every man or woman at death. But on the soil of Gettysburg there is something more we know about the dead. They died here not so much as individuals but as Americans; they died for the nation. Here the participatory power of memory arises especially strongly from the soil. If we have come as rememberers and not merely as tourists, particularly as American rememberers, then we must recognize these deaths as in one sense or another to be *for* us. The "consecration" of the ground Lincoln speaks of is now worked out fully and completely. For we have come upon sacrifice, sacrifice in death for life. And if we are Americans, we must know that the giving of these lives is directly tied to the lives that we now live.

The forces that converge on the ground of a place like the wheatfield in Gettysburg are powerful and primal. We do not need to place words on them to feel them deeply. Nevertheless, language is the next step, and it will come in one form or another. For it is by language that the sacrifice is drawn up into the life and understanding of the people for whom the sacrifice was made.

Here significant contests, new wars of words, almost inevitably begin. For the Philadelphia veterans, the erection of a monument in 1903 to "the man [Lee—a name the veterans could not bear to speak] whose statue it is proposed to place in honor upon the soil he desecrated and which the blood of our comrades made sacred" should be fought with a fury of phrases, like canister from a cannon.

It was Lincoln's calling, of course, to place words on the sacrifice. As we have noticed in his famous address delivered at the battlefield, he begins by acknowledging the poverty of his words in relation to the sacrifice of the lives given at Gettysburg. But by the stirring end of the address, the sacrifice has been put to use. It has become a rallying cry, a reason to redouble our efforts in war. By contrast, the second inaugural address carries another spirit. Between the two addresses lies Lincoln's own remembrance of what had gone before for the people he governed, namely, "the bond-man's two hundred and fifty years of unrequited toil." Moreover, this toil had not gone unnoticed by the God whose "judgments are true and righteous altogether." In speaking of this, Lincoln does not distinguish between one and the other side of the nation. Indeed, beneath we can see a form for the confession of a whole nation: What sort of people are we who would build an economy on the backs of our fellow human beings? Who are we that we have so quickly turned to shoot and stab those whom we a few years before embraced as fellows and brothers? As such a people, woe, horrible woe, is justly upon us all.

With these words the sacrifice on the wheatfield in Gettysburg and elsewhere throughout the land is turned not to new heroic efforts but rather to atonement. The blood spilt on the raging battlefield atones for blood spilt in the controlled but deeply violent pattern of life Americans—good Americans like the Berry family—had come to embrace in the many years prior to the war. Further, as the war wanes and we move on, the atonement and sacrifice open the way to the daily good work of living, not heroically, but carefully and well in the face of so troubled a past: "to care for him who shall have borne the battle, and for his widow, and his orphan." Perhaps in his reading and study of Jesus's words in Matthew or in the texts of the Old Testament such as Psalm 46, Lincoln came to understand that the great temptation for any nation is to turn the memory of the sacrifice of the lives of its men and women to grand purposes. If the nation is under God, if it can "cease striving" in this exalted way, lesser but truer goods can be cultivated and gathered in.

In a place like Gettysburg, the power of the memory of sacrifice remains palpable, even today. I believe this power can be shaped for the good as we visit and remember, or as we listen to and study words such as those of Lincoln, who later offered his own life in service of the people of whom he had been given charge. It will not be so shaped, however, if we do not walk the ground or if we do not listen and study. And of course, even then, there are no guarantees.

6

In the Country of the Savior

Death Comes for the Archbishop

I remember visiting the tomb of Oscar Romero, Catholic archbishop of San Salvador, in the summer of 2000. It was in the basement of the cathedral church in San Salvador. I was touring El Salvador with a group of faculty and staff from my university. Arriving at the cathedral, we walked around with a mix of reverence and curiosity among groups of Salvadorans scattered throughout the church. Some were worshiping, others were engaged in churchy sorts of tasks. A rehearsal of some sort was going on in one wing. I tried, with my very elementary Spanish, to listen in, but the confusion got to me. The church was big, but not so big to keep activity in one corner to itself. There were also renovations of some sort going on. I found it impossible to focus on any one thing.

I don't know how many people know about the crypt in the church. I certainly wouldn't have found it on my own. We followed one of our leaders down an unmarked stairway, which deposited us at the bottom into open, empty space. Renovations were also going on here. I believe they had been pouring cement—the wet smell of it lingered in the air. Romero lay, apparently, in a big cement box in one corner of the basement. The bodies of previous archbishops had permanent homes in slots in the wall; their various names were engraved there in order. Romero was twenty years dead, but, as we were told, there was hope that he might be canonized and so receive a more prominent burial place. Local church authorities were holding off on finding his body a final resting spot.

There was nowhere to sit in the basement. A few flowers and a stack of flyers lay on top of Romero's temporary tomb. I took one of the flyers and skimmed it, but there was nothing much in it I hadn't already heard. I recall standing in silence, not sure of what to do. My Catholic friends seemed similarly confused. Here we were beside Romero's tomb, but now what? No one was anxious to leave; however, if we stayed, was there something we were supposed to be saying or thinking or feeling?

The question remained unresolved for me. One of our number spoke briefly about Romero—by now all of us knew his story. There may have been a prayer. Soon enough we all left the cathedral and walked across the street. Here, on Cathedral Square, we found bustling life. A revivalist preacher, Bible in hand, stood on a bench. A crowd had gathered round. In another spot there was a skilled juggler. You had to shoulder in to see. Any number of booths dotted the large open area, each selling wares, including substantial Romero paraphernalia, along with Salvadoran flags, banners, and buttons, many of them strongly politically worded. Sometimes paired with that of Che Guevara (as if the two were best friends), Romero's visage gazed out from the T-shirts and flags hanging in the booths, impassively regarding the activity of the square.

Romero was killed by an assassin's bullet on March 24, 1980. He was presiding at a service in a small chapel kept by the Sisters of Divine Providence. The sisters, whose work was to care for the dying in their adjacent cancer hospital, had given Romero a small apartment to live and work in, and, in exchange, he said daily Mass for them. The Mass that day was being said for Sara Meardi de Pinto, who had died one year before. She was the mother of a publisher of a newspaper known for its courageous defense of El Salvador's poor. The Gospel text came from John 12: "the hour has come for the Son of Man to be glorified . . . unless a grain of wheat falls to the ground and dies, it remains just a grain of wheat; but if it dies, it produces much fruit. Whoever loves his life loses it, and whoever hates his life in this world will preserve it for eternal life. Whoever serves me must follow me, where I am, there also will my servant be" (14–16 NAB).

In his homily Romero spoke of Sara's readiness to live by this calling. Love of oneself could take over our souls, he thought, by "avoiding involvement in the risks of life that history demands of us." Those who try to "fend off the danger lose their lives, while those who out of love for Christ give themselves to the service of others will live, like the grain of wheat that dies, but, in death, lives. If it did not die, it would remain alone. The harvest comes about only because it dies, allowing itself to be sacrificed in the earth and destroyed."

Romero moved on to speak of the acts of hope and faith done habitu-ally and routinely by Christian women and men such as Sara, whose life had been lived in service. He concluded his homily with these words:

> This Eucharist is just such an act of faith. To Christian faith at this mo-ment the voice of diatribe appears changed for the body of the Lord, who offered himself for the redemption of the world, and in this chalice wine is transformed into the blood that was the price of salvation. May this body immolated and this blood sacrificed for humans nourish us also, so that we may give our body and our blood to suffering and to pain—like Christ, not for self, but to bring about justice and peace for our people. Let us join together, then, intimately in faith and hope at this moment of prayer for Doña Sarita and ourselves. (*Voice of the Voiceless*, 193)

At this moment a shot rang out. The bullet hit Romero full force in the chest. He fell down next to the altar and his blood spread over the floor. He was dead within minutes.

Ancient Patterns Repeated

Romero was archbishop during one of the most politically turbulent three-year spans in El Salvador's history. A mild man, somewhat book-ish, he surprised many by speaking out forcefully and repeatedly against the widespread government-sponsored oppression of the poor and its unbending and ruthless resistance to political opposition. In his short term as archbishop he gained the deep admiration and love of most Salvadorans, although he clearly angered the few rich and powerful who controlled the country—so much so that some decided he must be removed.

People flocked to Romero's funeral, which was held on March 30, 1980, on the Barrios de San Salvador, the Cathedral Square, where I, twenty years later, listened to the preacher and watched the juggler. Perhaps 150,000 people filled the space, including many church and political leaders from abroad. In the midst of the service, bombs sud-denly exploded in the crowd and government snipers stationed on nearby rooftops opened fire. Thirty people were killed, many more wounded. Romero's body was rushed into the cathedral, accompanied by terrified mourners who sought shelter in the church from the bullets. There it has remained in the concrete box in the basement.

Romero's story is extraordinary, eerie even. Clearly the assassin who shot Romero was uninterested in his words. He didn't wait to pull the trigger till right after the line about "giving our body and blood to suf-fering and pain, like Christ." He was merely looking for a clear shot.

As he spilled blood, he did not think about its power on the altar. And during the funeral, whatever person in power ordered that the bombs be set off and the troops to begin firing surely did not think about the uncanny relation: the death of the many as they gathered faithfully to remember the death of the one. Nor, I doubt, did anyone in the midst of their struggle for power and domination give much thought to the relation of Romero's death to the name of the nation they sought to control by violence: El Salvador—"the savior." In the country of the savior, the archbishop died a death that mirrored that of Jesus, whom he called "savior."

When I read back through accounts from the second- and third-century Christian church, passed down by Christian apologists like Tertullian, I find it hard to suppress a similar thought. When Roman emperors like Decius or Diocletian decided to kill some prominent Christians so as to persuade the rest of them to give up the faith and return to patterns of action and thought more fittingly Roman, did it occur to them or to any of their political advisers that killing Polycarp or killing Blandina actually gave the Christians a new group of "little Christs" to follow? Tertullian's adage "the blood of the martyrs is the seed of the church" is not quite self-evident, but also not rocket science. If you knew even the least bit about these Christians' stories, you would know that they followed after a man who was killed by governing authorities. If you were a governor who wanted to stop them, would it make good sense to kill again?

The uncanny logic we find in the story of Romero—strange on the side of the martyr, Romero, who dies like his savior, and strange on the side of the killers, the unnamed governors, who somehow don't notice the connection—may be sunk deep into the spiral of the human political pattern. One kind of power, the one we know the best, the power of *might*, always seeks its own ends. As it does, it destroys and kills. Romero's life, and Christ's, breaks with this power and displays another sort altogether, the power of *sacrifice*. One can notice all sorts of differences between the two powers, but for our purposes in this book, there is one we cannot miss. The power of sacrifice relies on a memory that the power of might has every reason to stamp out. When it tries to stamp out the memory of sacrifice, might often becomes stupid and forgetful, perhaps because of its dogged allegiance to its own ways. It cannot think in any other terms.

When Jesus is on the road to Jerusalem where he will be tortured and killed, his disciples start squabbling about who will be the greatest in the kingdom of heaven when it is established. He calls them to him and says: "You know that among the Gentiles those whom they recognize as their rulers lord it over them, and their great ones are tyrants over them. But it is not so among you; but whoever wishes to become great among you

must be your servant, and whoever wishes to be first among you must
be slave of all" (Mark 10:42–44). This passage extends the contrast just
made. Authority among the "Gentiles," or, simply, the "nations," relies
on might, and might seeks domination. "Among you"—that is, Jesus's
followers—there is to be a different dynamic, even if, as the disciples
have just shown, they themselves have a tendency to forget this.

The story of Romero plainly demonstrates the pattern of the power of
servanthood and sacrifice. Like the pattern of the power of might which
perpetually opposes it, the force of sacrifice is with us today, as both gift
and authority. Indeed, Romero's authority among the Salvadoran people
arises from service to the church and the poor for whom it cared. What
is especially striking, however, is his authority's range, which spreads out
beyond the church to the nation. This is due partly to the prominence of
the Catholic church in the nation of El Salvador. Romero was Catholic
archbishop of a very Catholic country.

I think, however, that it would be a mistake to identify the power
of the story of Romero in El Salvador entirely in terms of the relative
population of the church in the nation. Romero's is a Christian story, but
there is no reason to think that only Christians can know and recognize
its power, or tell it. In fact, the story rises up within the story of the nation and makes its presence known to anyone and everyone; it cannot
be ignored. If you are Salvadoran, Christian or no, the story is there in
the midst of your nation. Or, whoever you are, if you set about to tell the
story of El Salvador the nation, and omit the one about Romero, you
are covering over, misremembering, even lying.

Nations can neither control nor exclusively negotiate the stories that
rise up within them. Indeed, they are required in many cases to ride
along on the backs of these stories. What they ride on is nothing more
nor less than a kind of memory, one relating to the things we have been
speaking of throughout: land, birth and death, spilt blood, sacrifice. This
is true of America since 1863 or 2001, as it is of El Salvador since 1980.
There is a difference in El Salvador, to be sure. Romero died on the altar.
The men at Gettysburg died on the wheatfield, rifle in hand. Lincoln
died in the theater, and those in New York on September 11, 2001, died
on the job, at the very center of the dominating forces of world commerce. This makes it easier to tell and remember Romero's story in the
light of the blood in the chalice from which, as he finished his homily,
Romero planned to drink. But the fact that these others did not die on
the altar, their blood unmingled with the blood in the chalice, does not
mean the story of their deaths can be told separate from it. Romero's
story—not only the part about how he died but also how he lived and
what he said—helps us see how the sacrifice of a Christian martyr like
Romero on the altar, mirroring as it does the sacrifice of Christ on the

hilltop, relates to other sacrificial deaths such as those in the wheatfield of Gettysburg or even in the rubble of the Twin Towers.

Romero Writes as Pastor to His People

Romero assumed the archbishopric in February 22, 1977, two days after the national elections. These elections had been clearly fraudulent. Six days later, on the twenty-eighth, a demonstration protesting the fraud was held on Plaza Libertad in San Salvador. Soldiers opened fire, and the demonstration turned to massacre. Some fifty demonstrators were killed. Less than two weeks later, Fr. Rutillio Grande, a parish priest at Aguilares, a town outside of San Salvador, was murdered in his car on his way to say Mass—together with a young boy and old man who were traveling with him. As the film *Romero* portrays, Grande and Romero were good friends, and Grande's death touched his friend's soul deeply.

In response to Grande's murder, Romero ordered that a single Mass be celebrated at the Cathedral in San Salvador on the Sunday of March 20 and broadcast throughout the country on the radio; no other Masses were to be held anywhere in El Salvador that day. All Salvadoran Catholic eyes were to be turned in the same direction. This was a bold move; indeed, he issued the order in the face of the expressed opposition of the *nuncio,* the papal representative to the archdiocese.

We typically think of "church" as both local and universal, on either side of the middle space generally occupied in our modern times by "nation." In ordering the single mass, Romero stepped into this space, to the discomfort of both the papal representative and the national government. The effect of the move was to elevate the deaths of Fr. Grande, the young boy, and old man, to the level of representation. The remembrance of their lives and murderous deaths was a way to tell and remember the people's sufferings, which had been going on for years throughout the country under the repressive governance and economic oppression of the privileged few who controlled the national government. In this dramatic move, Romero signaled to his people that he would not let that part of the story remain untold.

The celebration of Easter came less than a month later, April 10, 1977. Romero determined that he should address the people of his church in the form of a pastoral letter entitled "The Easter Church." In that letter Romero returns to the story of Passover in Exodus. As remembered, this story was about Israel, but it opened up to other peoples as well. "God saves Israel, and thus it will be for every people, each within its own history." As the Jews understood, the celebration of Passover "was more than simply a remembrance of things past. The whole process of redemption was made present in a profound liturgical and sacramental, prophetic and eschatological, sacrificial and communal sense. There were lived out again the 'wonders' of the Lord" (*Voice of the Voiceless*, 55). The story of Passover, with its nub in the death of the lamb, has the extraordinary power to build up in the memory so as to gather people around it, in widening circles. "The immolation of the lamb conveyed a sacrificial and communitarian meaning, as did the gathering of the family or group, which patriotism later extended to take in the entire national community" (55).

Romero never advances a "theory" of the relation between church and state; theories are not the stuff of sermons and pastoral letters, which Romero hoped to keep accessible to all. But there may be another reason. For Romero, the stories of Passover and Easter had such power that they could not be contained. If the stories were told especially in the presence of suffering people, at funerals and baptismal Masses, or even in the midst of national holidays and gatherings, they would take hold and grow up into new life, like a grain of wheat in fertile soil. Drunk on theory, someone might imagine that proper political reason required that these stories be told only in church or synagogue. But particularly because Romero believed that the "church does not live for itself but so as to serve as Christ's instrument in the redemption of the whole of humanity" (57), he could not think of a church that was confined to one particular political space. Since the church served the people, where else could it be but out among the people of El Salvador?

"The Easter Church" turned out to be the first in a series of four pastoral letters issued from 1977 to 1979. The remaining three were issued not on subsequent Easters but on successive August sixths, in 1977, '78, and '79. (The string was cut short, no doubt, by Romero's death in March of 1980.)

Why August 6? It is the feast day of the Transfiguration and a national holiday for El Salvador. One might say that religion and nation both unite and face off in El Salvador on August 6. The Fiestas Agostinas—a carnival, really—runs for the week prior. On the feast day itself all the businesses and banks close, and a parade with floats passes through the streets of the city of San Salvador, ending at the steps of the cathedral, where the figure of Christ is symbolically lowered into the world. Thousands jam the Barrios de San Salvador, Cathedral Square, where the blood of the people flowed on the day of Romero's funeral.

As we have noted, Salvadorans' "patron saint" is none other than "El Salvador del Mundo" (the Savior of the World)—Jesus Christ himself. The Spanish Conquistador, Pedro de Alvarado, could not have known what he was putting people in for in 1528 when he piously dubbed the town that was to become a central city "San Salvador." The naming made the story of the preexisting church and the subsequent nation particularly difficult to separate. As Romero introduces his second pastoral letter, "Today the world's divine Savior, who is the patron of our local church, illuminates, with the splendor of this transfiguration—as at a Salvadoran Easter—the path through history of our church and nation. I believe it is opportune to write again to you who, together with me, make up this portion of the people of God who 'like a stranger in a foreign land, presses forward amid the persecutions of the world and the consolations of God'" (63, quote from *Lumen Gentium*, 8).

This introduction might appear to be a sloppy failure to distinguish between church and nation; it is in fact rooted in what Romero takes as an "insight, which runs throughout the pages of the Bible, into what God is doing in human history" (67). Put stubbornly, Romero is not prepared to relinquish the history of El Salvador to the nation of El Salvador. To do so would be to abandon its people, which the church, and Romero as its chief shepherd, is called to serve.

El Salvador is hardly a settled term. Its people are, in this quote, "like a stranger in a foreign land." This imagery fits well with the biblical story that lies behind the festival, which the Salvadorans on this day celebrate. In Mark's Gospel, Jesus goes with Peter, James, and John to the top of the mountain on a side excursion in the middle of the long journey from Caesarea Philippi to Jerusalem, where Jesus knows he will suffer and die. Jesus is doubly on the move. Moreover, when the group reaches the mountaintop, they are joined by none other than Moses and Elijah, rather notorious biblical travelers, both known for climbing mountains in foreign lands.

The vertical motion, the ascent up the mountain, matches with the imagery of transfiguration. When something is transfigured, it is changed—as the Gospels tell it, Jesus's clothes become "dazzling white." But transfiguration also suggests projection, as if on a wide screen across the sky. The particular becomes the universal; the strange Jewish man from the first century is suddenly savior of the whole world. As well, Jesus in the Gospels is transfigured into a community, joins a conversation, which runs between the Law and the Prophets, and beyond. This, as Romero puts it, is a path through history, one that cuts through his own nation. Moses, Elijah, and finally Jesus speak with the voices of the slaves and sufferers, those who otherwise have a strong tendency to go unheard in the national story.

It is in this context that Romero comes to speak of the "transfiguration of our people." This transfiguration of the people, says Romero, "is the traditional challenge to our homeland and to the church. It is unchangeable—as unchangeable as the truth and revelation of God. It ought to enlighten the realities of our history. We must learn to express it in the language spoken by persons of today" (4th letter, 114). In this quote, the "it," the "traditional challenge," is not quite clear until one reads back and forth through Romero's reflections in the four letters on the transfiguration scene. Repeatedly he returns to the voice of God that comes from the cloud: "This is my beloved Son. Listen to him" (Mark 9:7 NAB). So the Son, the transfigured one, has something to say; and the word of God on the mountain is that he must be listened to.

But who is he, and what is he saying? In his third letter, Romero works the point out explicitly. "To all Catholics, to our brothers and sisters in other churches, and to all persons of good will, we tell you that the Lord is present and this his voice speaks to us also from the misery of our people. Let us hear him: 'In so far as you did this to the least of these brothers of mine, you did it to me' (Matt. 25:40)" (111). So, the "traditional challenge" is hearing the voice of Christ in the misery of the people.

While this is a timeless task, it cannot be timelessly done. The poor we need to hear are the particular ones here with us. For El Salvador in 1977–80, it is its suffering people, the poor ones, the sick, the silenced, the "disappeared." This, then, is *their* transfiguration: they are lifted up on the mountain with Moses and Elijah so as to be heard. And for Romero, who was called to be their shepherd, there was no other option but to join with this voice of his suffering fellow Salvadorans.

> The foundation of all our work of evangelization is the mystery of Christ that we preach, the mystery that was so clearly revealed in the theophany commemorated by our titular feast. It has the certification of the Father, who presents Christ to us as the one and only Savior of the world. He alone is the way for the true liberation of Salvadorans and of El Salvador: "Listen to him." The church is his "body in history." We shall be more the church, and offer a better specific contribution from the church for the liberation of our people, the more we identity ourselves with him, and the more we are docile instruments of his truth and grace. (4th letter, 158)

This fourth pastoral letter was written in August of 1979 as the armed opposition to the military government strengthened, and so also the severity and brutality of the government's response. As 1980 began, El Salvador was moving ever closer to the full-scale civil war that would linger in the country for the next twelve years. On March 17, 1980, government and military response to the circumstances led to bombings throughout San Salvador, leaving sixty dead. Through the week the body count increased daily. On Sunday, March 23, Romero preached his last nationally broadcast homily. In it he stopped to directly address specific groups. First, he said he "would like to appeal in a special way to the army's enlisted men, and in particular to the ranks of the Guardia

Nacional and the police—those in the barracks. Brothers: you are part of our people. You kill your own campesino brothers and sisters. And before an order to kill that a man may give, God's law must prevail that says: Thou shalt not kill! No soldier is obliged to obey an order against the law of God. No one has to fulfill an immoral law. It is time to take back your consciences and to obey your consciences rather than the orders of sin."

Next Romero turned to those in power in the government, uttering the powerful words dramatized in the film *Romero*. "In the name of God," he proclaimed with great emotion, "and in the name of this suffering people, whose laments rise to heaven each day more tumultuous, I beg you, I beseech you, I order you in the name of God: Stop the repression!" (Brockman, 242). It was the next evening that the bullet ripped through his flesh, and his body slumped at the foot of the altar, his blood running over the floor as the Sisters of the Divine Providence rushed to his side, screaming in anguish and disbelief.

Romero's clearly was a prophetic voice. He does not place himself there on the mountain of Transfiguration with Moses, Elijah, and Jesus, but in retrospect it seems to me that *we* can, especially as we follow the point made above—that the voice of Christ is the voice arising out of the misery of the people. This is the voice Romero uses as he "orders" that those in power "stop the repression." Like a grain of wheat that dies, this is the same voice that continues to speak after Romero as his words are remembered, repeated, and built upon by the Salvadoran people. He signals this, in fact, in an interview a few days before his death: "If they kill me, I shall rise again in the Salvadoran people. I am not boasting; I say it with the greatest humility" (Sobrino, 41).

Nation and Church, Heroes and Martyrs

Sorting through Romero's *national* role as opposed to his *Christian* or *churchly* role would be an extraordinarily difficult business; in fact, it seems to me to be impossible. What we can say, though, is that Romero clearly held two things together: first, that nation and church were not the same thing, and, second, that the greatest service he could offer to them both was to speak for the suffering ones in El Salvador. The health of both the church and the nation depended fundamentally on the truth being told about the suffering and death of those Romero served. Without the voice of these, neither national nor church corporate life could continue as that, as life.

Since the transfiguration is celebrated in El Salvador as a national holiday, in that country it does very little to distinguish church and national life. It might, however, offer some visual clues about how the two corporate lives and memories might be differently projected.

The story of the transfiguration has its home in the story of Jesus, which has its home in the life of Israel. As Moses learns on the mountain (Sinai) and subsequently repeats to his people, Israel is to be to God "a priestly kingdom and a holy nation" (Exod. 19:6). The church's life extends this; it is, as Augustine says, a "city set on a hill." When he speaks with the voice of the prophet, the voice of Christ, Romero draws the lives and deaths of the suffering Salvadorans up into this life. They are transfigured. To extend the visual imagery to another hill, Golgotha, they are also crucified with Christ.

This lifting up of the suffering ones on Mt. Tabor or on Golgotha is not merely about their exaltation but also about their joining a company. In the transfiguration story, Moses, Elijah, and Jesus converse; if Romero is right to add the suffering Salvadorans as transfigured, they join this communal conversation that takes place above the earth in the high places. Transfiguration does not strike their names from the familial and national story in which their lives were lived, but it does place those lives into a different history, which extends through Moses, Elijah, Jesus, and beyond.

National life, even in a country called "The Savior," is not lived out on the high ground, but rather in the valleys—valleys like the Jezreel in Israel or perhaps even Rose's wheatfield in Gettysburg, where what feeds and sustains life on one day can be trampled and stamped to death on the next. Part of living this national life out well—part of fulfilling what we might call patriotic duty—is faithfully to remember the story of life in the valley. This includes especially the lives of those given in the valley in sacrifice for this valley life. National memory, however, is rightly confined to the valley. It cannot transfigure. Indeed, perhaps the greatest temptation for national memory is to carry its own valley life onto the mountain. As I have tried to suggest, this temptation is all the stronger when the touch with the fertile land upon which the nation's life depends—invariably valley land—is lost. Free of land, nation can become idea or grand experiment, and so it can imagine itself to be the eternal kingdom of God come to settle upon the earth.

The church is also not the kingdom, but its life depends entirely upon it. Its task is to make the kingdom present among the nations. From the story of the transfiguration, we might well learn of Peter's remark and the gospel's response that the church faces the opposite sort of temptation from the nation. You will recall that Peter babbles excitedly that the thing to do is to pitch tents on top of the mountain, in effect, to set up camp there. As Mark editorializes, "he did not know what to say" (9:6). But Peter is speaking out for a temptation of the church, namely, that it should stay on the mountain when it really needs to go back down into the valley where the suffering, but not the exaltation, takes place.

This proposal or attempt by Peter to keep things so nicely ordered on the mountaintop links with his attempt just a few verses earlier when, after telling Jesus and all within hearing that Jesus is "the Messiah," Peter does his best to keep his Messiah healthy. "Then [Jesus] began to teach them that the son of Man must undergo great suffering and be rejected by the elders, the chief priests, and the scribes, and be killed, and after three days rise again. He said all this quite openly. And Peter took him aside and began to rebuke him. But turning and looking at his disciples, he rebuked Peter and said, 'Get behind me, Satan! For you are setting your mind not on divine things but on human things'" (Mark 8:31–33). If Jesus is the true Messiah, and if the disciples who follow him are true disciples, they must come down off the mountain and continue on the way that leads to the cross.

This same point might be put another way. The transfiguration of the life of the church or of any community cannot be its own doing. God, not Romero, transfigures the Salvadoran people. It is something, rather, for which Romero prays: "Let us ask the divine Patron of El Salvador to transfigure in the same way the rich potential of this people with whom he has chosen to share his name. To be his instrument for bringing about this transfiguration of his people is the reason for the church's existence" (3rd letter, 110). Indeed, as we have seen, Romero moves in his fourth letter to a characterization of the church's life in terms of docility: "We shall be more the church, and offer a better specific contribution from the church for the liberation of our people, the more we identity ourselves with him, and the more we are docile instruments of his truth and grace" (4th letter, 158).

This docility is evident, I think, in Romero's comment to the reporter about rising again in the Salvadoran people—which he says with "humility." It is the mark of a martyr, who is, essentially, one whose reception of death is a witness to the truth of God's searing and purifying love. The church does not possess this truth, but it is ordered by it. (Put another way, in the truth, the church finds its reason to be.) And so the church produces martyrs who are, precisely, perfect witnesses to this truth about God. Although it is not built upon it, the nation can benefit from and even partly recognize this truth. Romero is not only Christian martyr; he is Salvadoran hero.

This is important as we move our focus in this book from the memories of nations to the memory of the church. Nations do not have martyrs; they have heroes, whose deeds they rightly remember, including their deeds of considerable sacrifice. The difference begins with the thing for which the hero or martyr gives his or her life, national life or the gospel, but extends beyond it to the way in which it is given.

In his discussion of fortitude in the *Summa Theologica*, St. Thomas Aquinas has back-to-back articles on fortitude and death. As Aristotle before him recognized, since fortitude (or courage) strengthens a person's mind against danger, and the greatest danger is death, then fortitude must indeed be chiefly about death. In fact, Aristotle says it is chiefly about death on the battlefield (ST II–II, 123, 5). However, the Christian Aquinas has something more to add, about both death and fortitude.

According to Aquinas, fortitude responds to the object of fear by doing something reasonable in relation to it—it neither rushes rashly toward it nor flees; rather, it takes stock of fear's object and responds. These reasonable responses of fortitude to fear's object can be two: aggression or endurance. Courageous aggression, Aquinas says, moderates daring—the passion closest to what we might today call "thrill." It does so by taking counsel, as did General Lee on one side and General Meade on the other—and then attacking, with appropriate daring.

Now, Aquinas thinks that to moderate daring (not to be rash), is not so difficult in the face of justifiable fear, for instance, when one's life is threatened. For fear already tends to moderate daring. When our life is clearly in danger, as in war, we do not attack merely for fun. If we attack well, and under fortitude's guidance, we are heroes. This is not to say it is easy being a hero, but Aquinas thinks it is the easier part of fortitude.

The harder thing to do in the face of fear is to wait. Attacking releases the anxiety of waiting. The more difficult part of fortitude, says Aquinas, is to endure, since endurance does nothing in the face of the justifiable object of fear except to stand fast. So, Aquinas concludes, "therefore the principal act of fortitude is endurance, that is to stand immovable in the midst of dangers rather than to attack them" (ST II–II, 123, 6).

So it is that martyrdom, which principally involves endurance rather than attacking, replaces Aristotle's death on the battlefield as the chief act of fortitude, at least according to the Christian Aquinas. Unlike aggression, endurance is served by patience. This combination, endurance and patience, demonstrates that the victory for which the martyr gives her or his life is fundamentally different from victory on the battlefield. After all, victory of one nation over another in battle, in the end, mainly secures land. This is no small thing: land, as we have been suggesting, is precious. Nations draw their life from it, and it roots their memories. The victory of the martyr, however, lies beyond and above land—one is tempted to stay on the mountaintop where transfiguration is wrought.

The faith and patience that the martyr displays is tensed: it lives (and dies) *forward* to the kingdom yet to come. The martyr is first and foremost a citizen of the coming kingdom of God. Christians call this "eschatological." The full reward of the martyr's death is not now but in the future. This future is in one sense impenetrable; we live toward it in faith and hope, the two of the three theological virtues that will disappear when we "behold him face to face." (Love will remain, since the one we will behold is none other than love unbounded.) But in another sense the future is here with us now, as no one sees more clearly than the martyrs themselves. Romero hopes—no, he seems actually humbly to *know*—that if they kill him, he will rise again in the Salvadoran people.

Back on Cathedral Square in San Salvador, Romero's memory has been mixed into national life. There his story is told, even if incompletely, on the T-shirt where his image is entwined with Che Guevara's. Across the way, in the cathedral's crypt, his body lies in a cement box, waiting to return to the earth in a place the debates and arguments of others will determine. On the anniversary of his death, many cram the square; his words are repeated and a Mass is celebrated. No one in El Salvador will forget him, even if many might prefer to. El Salvador, like many nations, is on an uncertain path, pulled in too many directions as it strains to keep up in the modern world.

Fr. Ignacio Ellacuria once said in a homily that "with Archbishop Romero, God has visited El Salvador" (Sobrino, 53). The comment suggests a descent, from the mountain to the valley. A few days after this homily, Ellacuria was martyred, one of six Jesuit priests who were killed, together with their housekeeper and her daughter, on November 11, 1989, at San Salvador's University of Central America, a few miles from the little chapel where Romero had been gunned down nine years earlier. One might take Ellacuria's death as counterevidence to his claim. Nine years later, what had changed? For Christians who remember, the claim points not only toward the sort of life lived in the valley, but back upward to the mountain where, as Romero would have it, the transfiguration of a suffering people is the pattern. And this pattern rests upon the suffering of the one whose death is said to bring eternal life, Jesus Christ, "El Salvador del Mundo" in whose memory the church finds its reason to be, its very life.

Part III

Church

7

In Moses's Memory

A Jewish Wedding, before and after September 11

At the University of Scranton, where I teach, we are lucky enough to
have a rabbi on our faculty in theology. In the summer of 2000, he did us
the favor of getting married. We knew this would be good for him but had
little idea how good it would be for us until the invitations arrived in the
mail. Everyone was invited to New York City for the whole affair: hors
d'oeuvres and opening celebrations, an Orthodox Jewish service, dinner
at one of the most famous and exquisite restaurants in Manhattan, and
a party afterward, including some serious Jewish dancing. Rabbi Marc
had foreseen that some of us would feel out of place during this dancing,
so he targeted our table of shrinking Christian theologians, grabbing us
each by the arm and swinging us into the sea of black hats surging over
the dance floor. I shall never forget finding myself suddenly shoulder
to shoulder with three Orthodox Jews as the four of us hoisted a chair,
Marc perched upon it, to shoulder height and bounced him about in
the bobbing black sea. Clapping and shouts of joy in Yiddish, Hebrew,
and English mingled with the accordion band; the walls shook and the
building swayed as we thumped and jumped about the room.

There are a great many more details to tell to complete this story of
Jews and Christians celebrating a happy occasion. Yet I will add only

one: the wedding and party I have described took place in "Windows on the World," on the 110th floor of World Trade Tower 1.

Without this last thing I would have gone on remembering my friend's wedding fondly for some time, but gradually it would fade. With it, though, it is one of those few events in my life that I shall never forget. For a new, powerful event has slashed across my memory of it, entirely reordering its significance. Quite simply, I cannot remember my friend's Jewish wedding without at the same time remembering images of hurtling bodies, consuming flame, and the smoldering, twisted heaps of metal to which Windows on the World and the rest of the World Trade Center were reduced on September 11, 2001. No doubt the bodies of many of the nameless ones, those who a year before had carried to us plates of caviar or cleared our tables while we danced and sang were buried amid those heaps. I cannot really remember them—their faces or their brief, polite words—but they, together with the rest of that horrible story, have *retrained* my memory of the Jewish wedding.

What does it mean to train or retrain our memories? One way to understand memory training is as the sort I did as a child in Sunday school. I worked hard to arrange all those Elizabethan English words like a line of train cars in my mind so that when my mouth opened they would file out in perfect order. This is memory work of a certain sort: memorization. Yet as the Jewish wedding at the top of the World Trade Tower illustrates, the memories that run the deepest in us are of a different sort. Training these will involve not so much producing by rote a string of words or images. Neither will it be just a matter of recalling details of past experiences, as some of us do well, others poorly. Rather, it will involve ordering our memories, remembering some things in the light of other things that are of greater significance. As my memory story suggests, we do not fully control how this ordering goes.

This may be where the training comes in. When we are trained well in something, it becomes part of us, and conscious choices are not so important. Often we can see the significance of the training only when we think of how it might be otherwise. Suppose we imagine a person who forgets or discounts the horrific destruction of September 11 and yet keeps keenly in mind—refers to and continues to revel in—the names and taste of all the many exquisite appetizers served at the wedding feast. Something is wrong with such a person's memory, we will say. It has not been rightly trained.

Yet how do we know what things should form other things in our memories? How do we learn to be a people whose memories are well ordered? I want to suggest that this takes long practice and is something that cannot be done alone. We need a community of memory. Family and nation are in one sense such communities. Our growth and development as bodies and persons is marked in terms of family, and they proceed in the context of the nation that presides over the land that sustains us. Both communities are mingled into our memories of this growth and development. In families and nations we keep a communal record, in story form, of where we have come from and where we are going.

If it stands alone, this story of birth and death, growth and decline, always circles back around to itself. The memory we keep is always ours, and we keep it for us. In a war, for instance, it is not a surprise that we tell the story as families differently if our children were killed in it. And likewise, as nations, we keep the number of our dead in a different column from theirs—like Paul Tibbets, whose flight over Hiroshima we Americans sometimes describe as the heroic act that saved one million American lives. So while we can receive good training within a family or nation to sketch out history in relation to family or national events, we may have difficulty reaching critical and truthful judgments about them.

September 11, 2001, is a national event that has begun to work its way into the national American memory. How will this go for the nation? We might begin, as we did in this book, by noting how we are tempted, perhaps especially in current times, to a "remembering" that is really a kind of forgetfulness since it turns everything into an adventure or thrill. If, like Odysseus, we wander the earth alone looking always only for the next adventure, every part of it comes to look the same to us. The earth becomes like Poseidon's untamed ocean. Ties to family, land, and community are sufficiently loosened such that one event and the next are all the same adventure.

For instance, a thoroughly modern Odysseus might decide to wear a T-shirt that says: "I survived 9/11/01 in NYC."

While this might be a tempting way to think of some events in recent US history, 9/11 seems to have awakened another sentiment within most Americans, one that connects to "sacred" things. I read a newspaper report that there was such a T-shirt in the early days following the attack—although I recently searched the Internet for it in vain. (The most common T-shirt design available on the Internet about 9/11 reads: "Gone but not forgotten.") We should not underestimate the power of capitalism to turn "Ground Zero" into a tourist stop. Yet most Americans see, and will continue to see, the "I survived . . ." mode of remembrance as offensive, myopic, self-centered, and cyclopean rather than human. As a nation, America wants rightly to remember 9/11; it feels a moral duty, even, to do so well.

We cannot assume, however, that so long as it is heartfelt and sincere, every way of remembering a national event like 9/11 is the right way. What is the right way? I'm not sure. Like the controversy about the

Enola Gay at the Smithsonian, we should expect disputes. Suggestions are better made concretely, and by analogy. About America's wars, for instance, I have recommended that if you are on your way to Reading, Pennsylvania, in June to see WWII, you might want to stay on the highway and go the extra few miles to Gettysburg, where you can get out and walk over Rose's wheatfield. Or, if you're standing at the Lincoln Memorial and are moved as you read through the rousing end of the Gettysburg address, you might also want to walk to the other wall and read thoughtfully through the second inaugural address.

We can anticipate objections. "Gettysburg is boring," someone might say, "and all its heroes are dead. I'd rather shake the hand of Paul Tibbets. . . ." I have tried to suggest why such a view might not be the best. Memory should touch the land, or be aware of fear and death and sacrifice. But even if such features are honored, we cannot assume disputes will be settled or bad memories made good.

Disputes about national memory will almost invariably involve disputes about God. God is invoked or drawn up into almost any national story I know, as El Salvador shows us perhaps even more clearly than does America. It may be a very difficult thing to tell and remember corporate stories about what a people have done or endured without also telling a story about God. The question, of course, will be: which god?

This question may be unsolvable on a national level, especially since any solution, if real, will demand action, not just words. As I have suggested, belief in one sort of God in America might entail that we all kneel and confess our sins.

It is not likely that most Americans will warm to such a God. Yet for anyone who is a Christian or Jew in America, or some other nation, some crucial things about how the "which God?" question are settled. This means as well that certain parts of the the "what and how should we remember?" question are settled. For Christians, no memory is more important than one particular one: Christ on the cross. In fact, all memories—be they familial, or national, or personal—must be held in mind, their stories told, in relation to this key one. Christians cannot go to Gettysburg or Reading or San Salvador or New York City without the cross. Similarly, Jews are held fast. In all that they remember, they must also remember Egypt and Sinai, Passover, exodus, and law. This is what makes both of these peoples potential aliens in any land where they settle. Never can the stories that arise from the lands they inhabit, from the soil that nourishes their own bodies and their children's, assert dominance over one or the other of these two stories. Put another way, man shall not live by bread alone. National and family life, the life of the soil, must accommodate the life of God. When it does not it needs to be left behind (the aliens move along), or its ways directly opposed, even to death.

Of course all of this is easier said than done, especially since the intermingling of familial and national stories and memories with the key stories and memories kept by Jews and Christians is a very natural sort of thing. Family and national stories are rightly about nurturing and sustaining life through time, and Jews and Christians affirm this life deep within their sacred stories. It is the easiest thing in the world, then, to simply fold the central stories of the exodus or the cross into our national and familial stories. How is this avoided? How are these two people to keep their memories straight?

Moses Teaches the Children of Israel How to Remember

Jews, I believe, have a head start on this problem. After my experience at the Jewish wedding, rightly or wrongly, I hold the opinion that it would not take too long to learn all that Jews could teach me about dancing. I had the sense that I was carrying Rabbi Marc on our shoulders just about as well as the Orthodox Jews who had enlisted my support in their dance. But Jews have more than dancing to teach. For instance, there was a great deal underneath the dancing, lessons about joy and celebration, that I thought I might learn, and this would take some practice. Likewise, and perhaps related to joy, there is a great deal to be learned, I am sure, from Jews about memory. Theirs is the longest living memory the human race knows.

Yet good memory is not just about longevity. It is also about honesty and truth. It is interesting to recall the family and national stories discussed in the first few chapters of this book: Jacob's sons or David's sin. Somehow, Israelite stories of family and nation remain frank and honest about the failure of prominent families and, really, the whole nation of Israel. These are family and national stories with an edge. What sort of training did the Jewish people and families have that produced such stories as these?

Their main teacher in these matters was Moses. In Torah he sets about to teach the children of Israel how to remember well. He does this most especially in Exodus, chapter 12, as he gives out important instructions to the people about Passover.

Reading Exodus 12

The progression of the narrative in the early books of Exodus is slowed almost to a standstill in Exodus 12. In previous chapters the nine plagues have been building rapidly upon one another; we feel we have reached the full crescendo as we are introduced to the startling tenth plague, the killing of the firstborn. As chapter 12 opens we breathlessly anticipate the coming of the terrible angel of death. But the angel is delayed for 28 verses while Moses passes on some rather tedious instructions about how to cook.

This first verse in the chapter displays a newfound concern about month and day and progression of the year. *"The Lord said to Moses . . . 'This month shall stand at the head of your calendar; you shall reckon it the first month of the year. Tell the whole community of Israel: On the tenth of this month every one of your families must procure for itself a lamb . . .'"* (vv. 1–3 NAB). In the progression of the nine plagues before this one, we have heard nothing much about time, unless perhaps an occasional reference to "in the morning" or "after seven days." The nine plagues have mixed together in a kind of monotony of calamity that relates temporally to little else but itself. The repetition actually numbs us to time and confuses our memory. (For example, I find it a challenge to recall the proper progression of the first nine plagues. There was the one about flies . . . but was that before or after the one about frogs?)

Yet we do not forget the tenth plague, as Moses insists. Once he has located us securely in the calendar, he offers instructions about the lamb, how it should be killed, what should be done with its flesh and blood, and so on. Then he says the following:

> This day shall be a memorial feast for you, which all your generations shall celebrate with pilgrimage to the LORD, as a perpetual institution. For seven days you must eat unleavened bread. From the very first day you shall have your houses clear of all leaven. . . . On these days you shall not do any sort of work, except to prepare the food that everyone needs. Keep, then, this custom of the unleavened bread. Since it was on this very day that I brought your ranks out of the land of Egypt, you must celebrate this day throughout your generations as a perpetual institution. (14–17 NAB)

The word *perpetual* puts us in mind of perpetual motion machines, which infinitely repeat the same movement. Like the first nine plagues, *perpetual* has a numbing effect; times before, now, and ever afterward indistinguishably meld. Yet here we have a "perpetual *institution*" that recurs on a particular day in a particular month, which means that it is *not* on all the other days in all the other months. As a particular day that is unlike any other day surrounding it, its effect is the reverse of a perpetual motion machine. It actually divides time—it makes a before and an after.

We get clearer about the perpetual nature of the institution with Moses's final set of instructions, given just as the night of the Passover darkens over Egypt:

You shall observe this as a perpetual ordinance for yourselves and for your descendants. Thus, you must also observe this rite when you have entered the land which the Lord will give you as he promised. When your children ask you, "What does this rite of yours mean?" you shall reply, "This is the Passover sacrifice of the Lord, who passed over the houses of the Israelites in Egypt; when he struck down the Egyptians, he spared our houses." Then the people bowed down in worship, and the Israelites went and did as the Lord had commanded Moses and Aaron. (24–28 NAB)

With these words the twenty-eight-verse interlude concludes, and the action resumes. Next words: "At midnight the Lord slew every first-born in the land." Yet there is much to comb back through, especially if we hope to learn something from Moses about memory. So that it will be easier to remember, let me put what I think he might be teaching us in characteristic Mosaic form: five commandments, the first tablet of memory.

The Five Commandments of Memory

Here, then, are the five commandments of memory:

1. Thou shalt rightly mark thy calendar;
2. At appointed times thou shalt stop working and begin celebrating;
3. Thou shalt assemble and eat together;
4. As thou dost assemble and eat together, thou shalt follow certain sorts of peculiar rules;
5. Thou shalt listen for thy children's questions and answer them.

Let us consider each of these in turn.

1. Thou shalt rightly mark thy calendar.

As we have seen, Moses's concern with time and calendar as the tenth plague approaches distinguishes it from the other nine, which appear by comparison as a muddle of troubles. The tenth plagues steps forth as if the only plague, unique in its *singularity:* one child, the first, from each family. And the angel of death does not pass over many times, but just once.

Singularity counts with memory. My father died about five years ago. I have thought of him often since. I have pictured him doing characteristic things, such as tending his rose garden or building a fire. Yet in August, I remember particularly his death. This was the time it came, as the summer waned. I suspect August will forever be marked for me in this way: as the tomatoes ripen and our children voice their dread about returning to school, I shall think of my father's death. He built many a fire and grew many a rose, but he died only once. It happened in August; and I shall always remember it so.

My father's death was a singular event. However, it is not its singularity alone that causes me to mark it. For instance, last February I made my first and only trip to San Antonio. Lovely though it was, I did not pause this year in February to remember it. My visit to San Antonio and my father's death are both singular events in my life, but my father's death holds a different sort of singularity.

We might think this obvious. But is it necessarily so? I can imagine a man for whom one singular event, say, visiting Disney World or winning the lottery, is more memorable than the death of his father. Yearly, on the anniversary date, this man looks back to features of his special event, to the ride on Magic Mountain or the numbers printed on the lottery ticket, with a sense of thrill or longing.

This man may be remembering quite well, that is, with exquisite accuracy, down to the exact number on the lottery ticket or the particular wild thrill he had while flying through Magic Mountain. Yet according to Moses, this man has not marked his calendar well. He has written things on it that do not belong, and left off other things that do. As Moses instructs the Israelites, whether they know it or not, *this* time, the time of Passover, must be a time above all times. All that they otherwise do or remember must relate back in some way to it: *"you shall reckon it the first month of the year"* (v. 1 NAB).

2. At appointed times, thou shalt stop working and begin celebrating.

If the calendar is rightly ordered according to Moses, it is marked permanently with such a phrase as "on this day God delivered the people from slavery" rather than "on this day I first visited Disney World." Yet once the day arrives, what shall be done on it? In Exodus 12 we hear a great deal about food: preparing it, eating it, and so on. Food, in fact, is in various ways the subject of memory commandments 2, 3, and 4. Number 2 clears the way: if we are to begin celebrating (and feasting) we must stop working. *"On these days you shall not do any sort of work"* (v. 16 NAB).

Not working is mentioned in the real commandments, the ten famous ones Moses later holds aloft on the stone tablets. Number 4 says: "Remember the Sabbath day, and keep it holy." The reason given there

(Exod. 20:11) is rooted in the creation story where God is said to have "blessed the seventh day and hallowed it, because on it God rested from all the work that he had done in creation" (Gen. 2:3).

Sabbath rest is difficult to understand in the modern world, for we tend to think of rest, especially on the weekend, primarily as a break from work. We go to work for five days, then leave, shutting the work door behind us, to go home to rest and relax—to play and do as we like. So understood, rest and work are the absence of one another. The biblical understanding, however, suggests a different relation. Work is formed by rest, and rest is formed by work. Rightly understood, memory is the glue that holds them together. Ceasing work does not mean forgetting it. God did not forget his work of creation as he rested on the seventh day. As God rested on that day, he was not taking a break; rather, he was looking back over—remembering—the work of the preceding six. This is important not just for understanding the rest but also the work. If work is to have meaning and sense, what we do in our rest must relate to it. This is what celebrating does. It turns our attention to something worthy. Work well done is such a thing.

Importantly, to Moses, the content of the work matters. Peoples celebrate different sorts of great works: victory at war, or the birth of a great hero. But Moses wants us to remember and celebrate God's work of deliverance from slavery in Egypt. For him, what we celebrate and remember will make us a different sort of people; it will indelibly mark our characters.

3. Thou shalt assemble and eat together.

When we celebrate what has been done in the past and that we now remember, we almost always eat. Indirectly, then, eating is related to remembering through celebration. But for Christians (and Jews before them) there is a more direct connection. A clue lies in the fact that when we eat, we *partake*.

Terence Fretheim notes in his commentary on Exodus 12 that the "Jewish liturgy for Passover stresses that worshipers in every celebration are actual participants in God's saving deed: God brought *us* out of Egypt. The Passover also serves as an important background for the New Testament presentation of the death of Jesus and the understanding of the Lord's Supper" (169). Food and drink are held aloft in celebration at Passover or at the Lord's Supper. As Christians eat the Supper again and again, we take part in the common body of Christ, the church. As we eat we are joined in the history of that body, which becomes present to us in memory.

Eating is the clearest and most material form of this sharing. Its symbolism in the Christian Eucharist seems spiritual and lofty. Yet it is also very ordinary and mundane. Eating, after all, is a very ordinary and bodily need that drives us together, as it appears to have driven the Israelites together for the Passover supper in Egypt. Moses instructs: *"If a family is too small for a whole lamb, it shall join the nearest household in procuring one and shall share in the lamb in proportion to the number of persons who partake of it"* (v. 4 NAB). Scarcity and shared need do not by themselves create community. In fact, they can break it, for hungry people often fight over food. But by Moses's command we join together. Once together, we cannot but notice that our needs are shared. Like the disciples tensely eyeing Jesus as he joined them at table after the resurrection, watching another person eat gives us assurance that we are alike.

I suspect this recognition of likeness has something to do with the way in which conversation issues from food. It often begins with the food itself, its smell or flavor. But soon stories are told, memories are shared, and what is past becomes present once again at the table.

4. As thou dost assemble and eat together, thou shalt follow certain sorts of peculiar rules.

This connection between eating and remembering and reciting stories is hardly unique to Jews and Christians. Odysseus, for instance, tells a major portion of *The Odyssey* to the Phaeacians after dinner. But Odysseus was not eating Passover with the Phaeacians, and he was not recalling the story of God's deliverance of the people from slavery in Egypt. The difference in the Jewish memory is marked not only by the distinctive company kept and the stories told, but by the food eaten and the rules about how to eat it. Rules such as: *"[you] shall eat [the lamb's] roasted flesh with unleavened bread and bitter herbs"* (v. 8 NAB). At the very least, this introduces a great deal of precision into the menu.

In our house you can always tell when it has been my turn to cook by the state of the kitchen afterward. This is a good deal because I cannot be bothered to follow a recipe. With a few notable exceptions (remembered in family lore), my efforts generally result in something quite edible, even tasty. However, I never cook the same thing twice; my sloppy style prohibits it. Food preparation for the Jews cannot be such a sloppy affair. They are people who are required to be quite precise about what is eaten, and this relates as well to being precise about what they remember.

Even today, in the Jewish celebration of Passover, there are distinctive foods to eat, like horseradish as the "bitter herbs," and distinctive times to eat them. With our potluck style, we Christians prefer spontaneity in our meals. I recall a youth leader in the 1970s telling our group at church that, really, you can have Communion with anything at all, even Fanta orange soda and pretzels. Perhaps he meant to make some sort of point that "Communion" is shared when we eat and drink anything together. Yet how would the Eucharist be carried from one generation to the next if the church adopted this youth leader's enthusiastic sloppiness? There can be room for deviation and innovation in a community's ritual life, but specific words and times and substances matter and set a pattern we will not easily forget. It becomes a part of us, and we of it.

If we are to be a people who carry and are carried by a story that is genuinely different, if our main narrative does not involve, say, Odysseus's clever escape from Poseidon's cave but rather God's redemption of the world in the death and resurrection of Christ, then the distinctiveness of this memory must work its way into our daily practices. The distinctive memory will be marked by the peculiarity as well as the precision of the practices. Eating is one such practice. In the Passover meal, the distinctive story Jews remember and tell is folded into the very food they eat. The precise pattern of the food accents the precise pattern of the story that is remembered. Following it sets the rememberers apart.

5. Thou shalt listen for thy children's questions and answer them.

The peculiarity of the food at Passover has something to do with the fifth commandment of memory derived from Exodus 12—when the children ask the questions. *"When your children ask you, 'What does this rite of yours mean?' you shall reply . . ."* (v. 26 NAB). In the sequence of the chapter, these words come directly after the instructions about sprinkling blood on the doorposts. While doing things around the house with animal blood was likely more common in Moses's day than in ours, surely this ritual was rather odd even then. The oddity is important; it captures attention, and occasions questions, particularly from children. Likewise, with food, I suspect bitter herbs will draw forth more questions than will mashed potatoes. "Yecch," says a child, "This tastes horrible! Give me one good reason why I should eat it."

We usually don't need to give reasons to someone, child or adult, as to why we eat things like mashed potatoes. Merely sitting down at table with our children will not bring out their questions, only their forks. Our common human need and desire for food makes the point of eating obvious. Similarly, we do not need to explain to our children why we engage in such practices as building houses or making money. Rather, at the dinner table or elsewhere, to draw genuine questions from our children, we need to be doing something sort of odd, something that does not contain its own explanation.

Jesus seems concerned about something like this in the Sermon on the Mount. *"But I say to you, Love your enemies and pray for those who persecute you. . . .For if you love those who love you, what reward do you have? Do not even the tax collectors do the same? And if you greet your brothers and sisters, what more are you doing than others? Do not even the Gentiles do the same? Be perfect, therefore, as your heavenly Father is perfect"* (Matt. 5:44, 46–47). Like blood on the doorposts or bitter herbs on the plate, practices such as praying for our enemies will bring forth our children's questions. The answers, as Moses sees, can be found only in a distinctive memory.

Moses, Christians, and Our Modern Lives

It might seem like the good Christian thing to say that someone even greater than Moses has come, and that he freed us from the constraints of diet and memory such as those followed by Jews. However, the case would be hard to make. For Christ, like Moses, commanded us to remember.

> And when he had given thanks, he broke it and said, "This is my body that is for you. Do this in remembrance of me." In the same way he took the cup also, after supper, saying, "This cup is the new covenant in my blood. Do this, as often as you drink it, in remembrance of me." For as often as you eat this bread and drink the cup, you proclaim the Lord's death until he comes. (1 Cor. 11:24–26)

Jesus gives this command to his disciples at the Passover feast; it clearly recalls Exodus 12. For Christians, of course, Jesus becomes the paschal lamb. This means we will read and remember the story of Passover somewhat differently from Jews. Yet the deep connection remains. The Jewish remembrance at Passover will echo in our Christian remembrance of Christ. If we are to become better rememberers, we must ask about our worship practices, particularly about Communion. How are we faithfully responding to Christ's command to remember him in our worship life? Or are our practices in worship forming us, particularly our children, to be a people whose memory will hold?

But we don't just "hold" memories. They inform what we do and how we think. They guide our daily practices and remind us who we are. "Remembering Christ" means being the kinds of people for whom the cross matters every day, the kinds of people who live by it. This memory must take pride of place, as Moses wants Passover to function for his people. Following Michael Wyschogrod, Stanley Hauerwas has cautioned Jews not to remember the Holocaust in such a way that it displaces the memory of the Passover and the subsequent giving of the Law at Sinai (*Against the Nations*, 61–90). A similar caution may need to be offered to Christians about other such monumental events, such as (for American Christians) the event of 9/11, recalled earlier in this chapter.

Worship concerns our corporate life as Christians, as did Moses's various commands about Passover given to the Israelites in Egypt. This is a point easily obscured in modern life in the West, where we like to imagine that faith in God is a private matter. This is especially important when we consider how memory shapes not just me, but us, as a people. Some memories are our own, and they matter to us individually, such as the memory of my father's death in August, which likely will remain with me until I die. Yet, when I do, it will also die with me. Its force may be deep for me, but it is also narrow and contained. By contrast, public or shared memories have genuine power through time; only they can form and carry a people.

Here again, as modern western Christians we typically believe that character formation is a private matter—something families do. And clearly families form their children as well as birth them. But as Moses sees, within family, when our children ask us what is the meaning of the strange rites we introduce them to, we cannot answer merely in terms of some private familial story such as "This is the day your grandfather died." Rather, we must point their attention beyond family to God, who, on this day, brought us out of Egypt or, on this day, gave up his life to redeem us.

In the first of the five commandments of memory, where we "rightly mark our calendars," the interaction between family and the larger story is sharpened. As a parent living among other parents in modern America, I have the strong impression that our affection for our children is killing both them and us. There is no better place to see this than on our calendars. They are filled with activities specifically for our children: parties, sports, lessons, performances, recitals, etc. This is, of course, a familiar complaint among American parents, as we all vow to cut back on something next year. But such half-hearted resolutions fail to address the underlying problem, which is, simply, that we parents have come to believe that our children are the most important things in our lives. But this is idolatry. Moreover, our children actually do not want to be the most important things in our lives, and the fact that they are is killing them. Deep down, they would much rather be in a position to ask us about why we do what we do ("What does this rite of yours mean?"), and to join in.

Proper love for our children must point beyond them, beyond family, to God. Calendars can help do this. Jewish calendars typically do; Christian calendars might. The church year provides the evident framework. If we mark them rightly on our calendars, Easter and Lent direct our memories to the story we and our children must keep and retell, before we tell the particular stories of our children's achievements. And, again, this is as our children wish. For they know better than we do that their own achievements cannot sustain a world.

Calendars can display this pattern in ways other than by the church year. Some churches have established yearly traditions that are awaited with the anticipation of a great feast day. In my own congregation, last year the youth mission trip in June was repeatedly set before us, for funds needed to be raised for it. A garage sale in one month or a hire-a-youth day the next focused our corporate attention on what our youth did in June. This changed the rhythm of our year; it pointed more clearly than in other years to the continuing story of God's redemptive activity in Christ.

The second memory commandment concerns work and celebration. Here again the privatization of our imaginations is a hindrance. The practices that form and sustain a people to remember well are public and shared, but if we conceive of our work as something we do only for ourselves or for our family, stopping work to engage in these practices will have little meaning. I think Moses's instructions imply that celebration should turn our attention to work done well, the model, as we have said, being God's work in creation. We remember what has been well done or accomplished. So long as they are not thought self-sustaining, things we have done well are rightly celebrated.

Recently in my own church we began a search for a head pastor. To prepare for this we had to compose a "parish profile," designed both to attract prospective pastors and to assess the state of our own common life. Writing the profile moved us to celebrate the work that so many had done in years past to lead our congregation to its present place. This helped relate our own present work to what these other Christians had done in the past. This built our common life, reminding us what God had done to build us into a church. If we follow the command to cease our work—not just to take a break, but rather to celebrate God's work among us—we will better remember who we are in the context of this past work and pursue our own in its light.

The third commandment of memory involves assembling and eating. Besides what it implies about the Eucharist, I am absolutely serious when I say it should be taken to require church potlucks. The symbolism is almost as deep: each of us brings his gift humbly to the table (perhaps in an ugly brown casserole dish), we partake together, and later praise one another on the basis of how well we have been nourished. Beyond pot-lucks, recall also that Moses commands families to join in one another's homes to eat the Passover lamb, as directed by each family's needs.

A liability of living in a rich country like America or Canada is that many of us are not directly acquainted with someone who lacks food. We should be on the lookout in our local areas for those in such need, but they only sometimes can be found. However, there is another widespread need even, or perhaps *especially*, in our rich communities: a need for companionship. People are eating alone. Christian families can do a great deal here simply by asking others to dinner. When they come, memory will be much involved. First, at dinner, stories will be shared. But further, subsequent generations will later recall eating in a house with an open table. Such a memory will have a great deal to do with the continuation of hospitality and communion in succeeding generations.

The fourth commandment of memory flows together with the fifth. We are directed in the fourth to do odd sorts of things at our dinner tables, and elsewhere; and this oddity is what brings out our children's questions—which the fifth commandment tells us to answer. In both commandments we are directed to consider why we do the things com-manded in the first three: why we mark our calendars in the way we do, why we work and celebrate as we do, and why we assemble and eat together as we do.

It is sometimes said in America that "our children are our most im-portant resource." We also sometimes speak of them as our "hope for the future." These phrases are so common even among us Christians that we fail to note that they are blasphemous. This is not only because they make idols of our children, but also because they collapse the present into the future, forgetting that God is with us now.

Any people, if they are to remain a people, will need to sustain a com-mon memory. The sort of people that remain will depend on the sort of memory that is sustained. This—the character of the people—will depend not just on what is remembered, but also how it is remembered in the *present time*. Here we must see something about memory that I have implied throughout this book but never made explicit. It is that memory is as much, even more, about the present as it is about the past.

Augustine notes in book 11 of his *Confessions* that, strictly speaking, there is no past, present, and future, but rather a past present, a pres-ent present, and a future present. The past, as he says, is no more, and the future is not yet, except as it is held in our memories. This does not mean we sustain the timeful universe in our minds. That is up to God. However, it is a fearless Christian affirmation that we do indeed sustain the life of Christ in the world—this is not by our choice but by Christ's, who shares our life and makes us his body. Our memory of Christ's life, death, and resurrection, therefore, does not so much look back to what once was but rather affirms Christ's life with us now. The affirmation is ineffective if it is presented only as a story to be told. It must be enacted. The fourth and fifth commandments begin with our strange actions at the dinner table and elsewhere. These will bring questions from our children and perhaps disdain from the world. Yet if they are faithful, these actions will make sense in the context of the truthful recollection that not only did God rescue the Jews from Egypt, he also came to live and die among us in the form of the servant, Jesus of Nazareth, whose memory even now remains present with us.

8

A Dinner to Remember . . .
but Judas Leaves before Dessert

Two Brothers with Different Memories

The history of Israel is shot through with bodily continuity. Jews today who have listened to Moses and remember are joined not just in spirit but also in body with those who first celebrated the Passover as described in Exodus 12. For Israel, the connection between family and nation is not an object of speculation; it is assumed into the story from the start. Jewish memory is in many ways like family memory: it's not something you can opt out of.

People sometimes try to turn "being Jewish" into something like "being Scandinavian," with limited success. When they do this we usually feel a sort of sadness, partly because so many have died for being Jewish. As Stanley Hauerwas has said, if you're Jewish and you let your child "choose" about whether or not to have a *bar* or *bat mitzvah*, something has gone deeply wrong. Six million dead, and now we're letting kids choose whether to carry on being Jewish?

Jews may have the opposite problem from the rest of us. They remember almost *too* well—and the history lies heavily upon them. Yet the readiness of Jews to remember is a kind of service to us all. In so doing they anchor us all to the earth. This has implications for what Jews and Christians call the holy land, which was sanctified by sacrifices such as that Abraham offered for the covenant (Genesis 15) or the ram that took Isaac's place on Mount Moriah (Genesis 22). The land became holy because God chose Israel. Yet beyond this, because the Jews remember as they do, because their story ties the human race in a long unbroken line of struggle with God's presence on the earth, the memories the rest of us keep can loosen a bit. So while Christians must learn from Jewish memory, we need not replicate it in every aspect.

For instance, a quite justifiable fierceness about memory rises up in these Hebrew words from Psalm 137: " If I forget you, O Jerusalem, let my right hand wither! Let my tongue cling to the roof of my mouth, if I do not remember you, if I do not set Jerusalem above my highest joy." For the writer of this psalm in captivity in Babylon, Jerusalem has been taken away, and he cannot allow it. Forgetting is like letting the Babylonians (or the Nazis) win.

For Christians, there may be more room in our memory to forget, or, if not to forget, to open gaps in memory that can be filled with new things. For the church fathers, scripture was subject to levels of interpretation, including an *allegorical* level. This was subject to great abuse, of course, but also opened up the imagination. Suggestions of allegory get us thinking. Particularly in the reading of the Bible, allegory transfers a story or event into another time. It mixes times, preserving connection at the same time that it reinterprets and reorients.

Consider an allegorical reading of the brothers in the parable of the prodigal son we discussed earlier. The story is all about a new beginning for the prodigal, the irresponsible younger brother. But it does not leave out the older brother and, at its end, names his quite understandable dissatisfaction with the whole affair. The older brother has been long faithful, stayed with his father, and dutifully worked the land. He knows the intricacies of family life—surely he is well aware of his younger brother's impetuous ways and of his father's urge to make all things right. He cannot just overturn this past in a minute. So he sticks to it, tenaciously. Like the Jew that he is, he is ready even to challenge his father on a point of justice. By contrast, the younger brother has skipped off to wherever his pleasures led him, tried his best to forget his family, squandered his inheritance, and now, in the story, returns a penitent who is hoping for a fresh start. Like the younger brother, Christians look for gaps in memory that can give room for new beginnings.

The unbroken line of bodily continuity in Judaism is matched among Christians by talk of a *new* body, a *new* life. This emphasis has provided a base for the born-againism of modern Protestantism. Yet as many have pointed out, such an emphasis is in danger not only of losing its memory, but also of losing the corporate community who remembers. This corporate body is what Christians call church. The church is God's extraordinary experiment insofar as it is family and nation *transferred*. The language and relations of family, even of nationhood, are allegorized into the church. Christians are brothers and sisters in Christ; they are representatives of Christ and his kingdom. Yet the allegory becomes real in the church, which is, the Christians say, Christ's actual body in the world. As Dietrich Bonhoeffer so emphasized, the church is only the church as it *takes up space* in the world (Bonhoeffer, 68).

Taking up space means, for Bonhoeffer, that the church is not mainly about ideas or moving personal experiences but about a people who live and work somewhere together. You can go and find them: here it is—the church. The extraordinary puzzle for Christians in the church is to learn how to occupy space, to really live somewhere (which must include digging down into the earth, having and raising children, loving the particulars of some one spot), while at the same time knowing, as Augustine accents, that our true citizenship lies elsewhere. Christians' way of talking sometimes indicates this puzzle: we Christians are "resident aliens," or (as the *Book of Common Prayer* puts it) earth is our "island home."

That they see themselves as a new body in the world will to some degree change how Christians remember, as opposed to how Jews do. The line will be more jagged or dotted as we move with God through human history. There will be some surprises and apparent discontinuities. Practically, this will reorient how the communities we have been discussing, family and nation, are regarded. Jews, for instance, cannot dismiss the idea that a nation might yet be how Jehovah is representing himself to the world. This is because the bodily and familial continuity of the Jewish people has been, and may yet continue to be, extended into the world in the form of the nation of Israel. By contrast, for Christians who speak of the "new Israel," it should go without saying (even though it sometimes nonetheless needs to be said) that no particular modern nation-state can legitimately claim to extend Christ's body in the world. Whatever the church is, it is not the nation. Wherever the church takes up space, it cannot be simply the space circumscribed by the natural or artificial boundaries that divide nations or peoples from one another.

The proclamation of this view can and should create some consternation among the nations. Modern nation-states will want a god to remember by, for national life will require sacrifice and so invoke sacred memory. But Christianity has in one sense taken God away from the nation (and the household) and given him to everyone. We should expect a reaction. Indeed, the modern secular state is a kind of backhanded

Christian creation insofar as the church has maintained that no one people can claim they belong to Christ more than any other people. If it lives long enough free from this Christian discipline, the secular nation may go looking for its gods again. Secular nationhood may not be so stable an idea as it for the moment appears.

How can the church courageously and also delicately carry along the living memory of God's presence in Christ among the nations, particularly among increasingly secularized nations who yet long for a god to remember by? This is the extraordinary challenge for the church in our time. To see how this might be done well, we will need to consider more stories like Romero's, or perhaps Lincoln's, or Martin Luther King Jr.'s, or Pope John Paul II's.

However it is done, certain peculiar memories must remain central to the church's life. To return once again to the prodigal, even if he and his father begin life anew, he cannot forget where he came from and what he once was. Perhaps this will be his (and, by allegory, Christians') greatest temptation: to take his new life so for granted that he supposes he is no longer tied to what went before. Here the elder brother's reminder of what really has happened in the family is a needed hedge against deception. As the younger brother goes to the feast with his father, he cannot forget what the feast cost his family, or how his own earlier pride and pleasure led him to meals shared with the pigs.

Fortunately the key memory story for Christians, rightly told, will not allow us to forget the time before we were invited in to share bread with Jesus, who is God made flesh for us. Indeed, the story suggests that even in the midst of the meal we are quite capable of turning and abandoning it. Laced throughout the story of the passion and death of Christ, and particularly the story of his last supper with his disciples—the supper Christians reenact weekly following the command to "do this in remembrance of me"—is the truthful story of desertion, denial, and betrayal.

The Last Supper in Text and Context

In the *Book of Common Prayer*, which we follow like a map in our services at my Episcopal church, the words of preparation for communion on certain Sundays begin like this: "On the night he was betrayed the Lord Jesus took bread, said the blessing, broke the bread, and gave it to his friends and said, 'Take, eat, this is my body which is given for you. Do this in remembrance of me.'"

I had probably heard this recited a hundred times before one day I was suddenly jolted by the contrast in it: Listen to it again: *On the night he was betrayed . . .* Jesus took bread, broke it, and gave it to his friends.

I had always thought of the Last Supper as just the Last Supper. It is such a huge event in the Christian story that it doesn't need a context. But the phrase from the prayer book links it with something shocking: *betrayal*. If you look further in each of the four Gospels, they do the same. They put the story of the Last Supper in the middle of a story of betrayal.

I have wondered sometimes about how things went at that supper. When we get together to eat, we converse. Since they had been together so long, surely there was some banter between the disciples. Since banter always arises out of some shared memory, I can imagine, for instance, Andrew saying to Peter: "Remember that time when we saw Jesus walking on the water and you started to climb over the side. I thought: 'Peter! You idiot! You'll drown!'"

The Bible shows no real interest in this approach. Instead of portraying the supper as a cathartic community event when the group looks back on what it has been through together, it actually goes fairly directly after one person: Judas. Besides Jesus, he is the main player. Moreover, his response to a preceding event, when a mysterious woman anoints Jesus in Bethany, seems to provide necessary background for the events to follow.

This woman, like Euryclea in the story of Odysseus, seems to have some deep connection to remembering. Here is the whole passage from Matthew 26, beginning with the woman and ending on the Mount of Olives, where Jesus and his disciples go together after they have eaten.

> Now while Jesus was at Bethany in the house of Simon the leper, a woman came to him with an alabaster jar of very costly ointment, and she poured it on his head as he sat at the table. But when the disciples saw it, they were angry and said, "Why this waste? For this ointment could have been sold for a large sum, and the money given to the poor." But Jesus, aware of this, said to them, "Why do you trouble the woman? She has performed a good service for me. For you always have the poor with you, but you will not always have me. By pouring this ointment on my body she has prepared me for burial. Truly I tell you, wherever this good news is proclaimed in the whole world, what she has done will be told in remembrance of her."
>
> Then one of the twelve, who was called Judas Iscariot, went to the chief priests and said, "What will you give me if I betray him to you?" They paid him thirty pieces of silver. And from that moment he began to look for an opportunity to betray him.
>
> On the first day of Unleavened Bread, the disciples came to Jesus, saying, "Where do you want us to make the preparations for you to eat the Passover?" He said, "Go into the city to a certain man, and say to him, 'The Teacher says, My time is near; I will keep the Passover at your house with my disciples.'" So the disciples did as Jesus had directed them, and they prepared the Passover meal.

When it was evening, he took his place with the twelve; and while they were eating, he said, "Truly I tell you, one of you will betray me." And they became greatly distressed and began to say to him one after another, "Surely not I, Lord?" He answered, "The one who has dipped his hand in the bowl with me will betray me. The Son of Man goes as it is written of him, but woe to that one by whom the Son of Man is betrayed! It would have been better for that one not to have been born." Judas, who betrayed him, said, "Surely not I, Rabbi?" He replied, "You have said so."

While they were eating, Jesus took a loaf of bread, and after blessing it he broke it, gave it to the disciples, and said, "Take, eat; this is my body." Then he took a cup, and after giving thanks he gave it to them, saying, "Drink from it, all of you; for this is my blood of the covenant, which is poured out for many for the forgiveness of sins. I tell you, I will never again drink of this fruit of the vine until that day when I drink it new with you in my Father's kingdom."

When they had sung the hymn, they went out to the Mount of Olives.

Then Jesus said to them, "You will all become deserters because of me this night; for it is written, 'I will strike the shepherd, and the sheep of the flock will be scattered.' But after I am raised up, I will go ahead of you to Galilee." Peter said to him, "Though all become deserters because of you, I will never desert you." Jesus said to him, "Truly I tell you, this very night, before the cock crows, you will deny me three times." Peter said to him, "Even though I must die with you, I will not deny you." And so said all the disciples. (6–35)

Money and Memory

Peter is the only disciple who gets named in this account besides Judas, and his action principally involves what is done and said *after* supper, when Judas (according to John's account) has already left. Judas starts it all off early, making the deal with the high priests sometime in advance. The text gives us the impression that he is driven to it partly by what happened with the woman. The disciples taken together are displeased with Jesus—and in Matthew's next line Judas is talking to the high priests. I think we can assume Judas was one of those who got especially angry over the wasted oil. (In fact, in John 12:4–5, the word of objection comes explicitly from his mouth.)

What we find out in Jesus's subsequent exchange with Judas and the other disciples about what the woman did is that Jesus is definitely not a utilitarian. As we all get taught in an introductory course in "ethics," utilitarians are people who believe you should go around always maximizing the happiness of the greatest number. Perhaps Judas made the utilitarian argument to Jesus: this woman did not maximize happiness; she poured out good money on the ground. Jesus disagrees with this and praises the woman, something Judas seems to take personally. He and his Lord appear to have different ideas altogether about the efficient use of resources—about *money*.

Actually, we can expect Judas to have some views about money. After all, he kept the moneybag. In fact, in John's account of the Last Supper, when Judas leaves before dessert, the other disciples assume he is on some mission with money.

> So when he had dipped the piece of bread, he gave it to Judas son of Simon Iscariot. After he received the piece of bread, Satan entered into him. Jesus said to him, "Do quickly what you are going to do." Now no one at the table knew why he said this to him. Some thought that, because Judas had the common purse, Jesus was telling him, "Buy what we need for the festival"; or, that he should give something to the poor. So, after receiving the piece of bread, he immediately went out. And it was night. (John 13:26–30)

It is probably unhelpful, not to mention self-righteous and hypocritical, for someone in the modern "developed" world, someone like me, to talk too much about the evils of money. After all, whoever we are, we are always glad to get it. We find it exceedingly useful. Nevertheless, the fact that Judas is so much associated with it should make us pay close attention. Coming to this story with memory in mind may help us critically consider one of the great troubles that arises as we come to have money, or concern ourselves inordinately about how we might get more of it.

In the passage from Matthew above, Jesus speaks of his blood as "of the new covenant," and of his body "which is broken for you." To this last line, Luke adds, "Do this in remembrance of me" (Luke 22:19). In Paul's account in 1 Corinthians, this remembrance is accented. As he puts it, Jesus says, "This is my body that is for you. Do this in remembrance of me." And then, about the cup, "This cup is the new covenant in my blood. Do this, as often as you drink it, in remembrance of me" (1 Cor. 11:24–25). Of course Paul's words have had long effect, for the Christian church has since placed Eucharist (or Communion) at its center. It is one of those very few requirements at the core of the faith: remembering Jesus's death, and participating in it by consuming his body and blood, is *essential* for those who would call themselves Christians.

Since this is so central to the Christian faith, it should make those of us who are rich in the world just a little nervous that the account of the Last Supper in the Gospels concentrates on Judas, who seems unable to join in the supper partly because he has his mind on other things, money prominent among them. For our discussion of memory, here is a troubling implication: people who think about almost nothing but money—how to make it, where to spend it, how to maximize its use—are, to a person, lousy rememberers, at least in the sense we have been thinking of memory in this book. (To be sure, some such persons may be able to recall with exquisite clarity all the details of, say, the making of their first five dollars.) These people are mostly concerned with efficiency—and memory is in one sense quite inefficient.

Efficiency extended indefinitely (as it often is in our own time) creates a sort of infinite path of use, whereby one thing is used to get another thing, which is used in turn to get another thing, and so on. Memory might similarly be turned into an efficient thing: if you become good at it, then you might win a promotion, or gain influential friends. But that is precisely not the sense of memory we have been following throughout this book: memory is not what we use or control to become who we want to be, to go where we want to go. It is rather the stuff that holds us in the places we already are. If anything, memory puts us in our place and reminds us of how little we control, and of how much we are the subject of others' gifts and trials.

Particularly on this night with his disciples, Jesus knows that what lies ahead of him is what he must endure rather than what he will control. In this time with his friends he hopes to gather together a community that likewise will receive what the world throws at it, but will, nonetheless, remain firm in faith through the unpredictable future. His friends will be equipped to do this only as they remain as one and remember this night by eating together the body and blood of the one they call Master.

It is fitting that Judas leaves as he does at this point in John's account of the supper and goes out alone into the dark. He cannot be still; he cannot wait within the community of followers for what is to be endured and suffered. For Judas is a man with a plan. For him, sitting around chatting over dessert could be nothing else than a waste of time and money. Jesus senses this and tells him to be *quick* about it. Paraphrased, we might hear him say: "Judas, do what you do best: be *efficient*."

The Women and Jesus's Body

Judas dominates the story of the Last Supper, yes, but he has a foil. We do not know her name, but it is from her act that the story we have been telling springs. This is the woman who poured the costly ointment over the head of Jesus. As Jesus tells us in Matthew, we will remember her as often as we retell God's good news. In contrast to Judas, what she did was profoundly inefficient, which is precisely the basis of any sensible man's criticism of it.

I do not believe it is an accident—as it was no accident with Euryclea in *The Odyssey*—that she is a she and Judas is a he. Like Euryclea with Odysseus, this unnamed woman's contact with Jesus is bodily. Oil poured on the head embraces the whole of the body. This body, of course, is soon to hang on a cross. Subsequently, when it has been taken down and laid in a grave, another set of women arrives to do as this woman did: anoint it. This was "according to the burial custom of the Jews," John tells us (19:40).

As the Nazis and other such killers knew, almost all human burial practices are profoundly inefficient. In a completely efficient world, dead human bodies become a problem to be solved; no better indicator can be found of such "efficient" practices than the mass grave. Women, it seems to me, are less easily fooled by such comprehensive efficient plans that turn bodies into things.

I do not think this is unrelated to what we noted earlier in connection with the family. As we have suggested, the family is that unit of memory by which we are tied to the earth, and therefore to body, and therefore to what we have received rather than to what we later choose. All memory is in some way related to this first source. While men (like David) can come to know the power of intimate bodily touch and mourn its loss, women typically know it better.

The skills required for proper care of the body in the family, even care in mourning, are not unrelated to those Aquinas thought were required of martyrs. One must be ready to take the time, to receive what has come one's way and yet to continue to touch those whom one has been given to love. This is particularly difficult in times of uncertainty, danger, or, as in Jesus's case when this woman anoints him, impending death. The skill, in effect, is one of actively enduring, of keeping close contact with one another in the midst of danger and trouble. Our urges often push us to either side of this mark, either trying by violence and decisive action to take control or withdrawing into drowsy indifference.

In the garden scene we have men who miss the mark on both sides. On the one hand, we see Judas, who comes to work out the final stages of his plan. Just before he arrives, on the other hand, we see the other disciples, who remain with Jesus in the garden, overtaken by lethargy. Although Jesus tells them to watch and wait, they fall asleep (Mark 14:37).

It is perhaps a mundane example, but it has been the experience in our family household that while I sleep as if the world were not, my wife stirs restlessly until she hears the sound of our oldest son's return when he has gone out at night. Without generalizing or universalizing this phenomenon, I know from discussions with other families that it is not uncommon. More women than men can detect bodily presence;

they know better what patient endurance means, and how to watch and wait.

Euryclea is one example of this, but there are many others. The three Marys (Jesus's mother, Magdalene, and the "other Mary") and this unnamed woman with the ointment know how to treat Jesus's body. They point out to us what we might otherwise miss: Jesus is his body. (This is something the Docetists later try their best to forget. According to this early Christian heresy, Jesus only *appeared* to have a body. It couldn't have been an actual human flesh-and-blood body like yours or mine. For what sort of God would consent to that?) In contrast to the Marys, Judas uses the language of the body only as a sign, one he can twist and reinterpret: he betrays with a kiss. The woman's anointing and Judas's kiss . . . could we think of two more profoundly different acts?

Judas is joined on the side of efficiency by another male, one far more powerful. In John, when Jesus arrives in Jerusalem to prepare to celebrate Passover with his disciples, Caiaphas, the high priest, begins to plan to have him removed, saying, "it is better for you to have one man die for the people than to have the whole nation destroyed" (John 11:50). If Judas was a Zealot, as he is often portrayed in modern retellings of the story, he and Caiaphas represent opposite wings in the political debate of the day. Caiaphas's Sanhedrin meant to maintain the status quo under Roman rule, while the Zealots wanted it overthrown. Yet both thought in exactly the same way: how can we manipulate the present circumstances, use our money and time and power maximally, so as to bring about the outcome we want?

One might say that Jesus and his disciples get crushed between the efficiencies of Caiaphas's plot and Judas's betrayal. After the Last Supper they go up onto the Mount of Olives and obliviously sing a hymn while Caiaphas and Judas, each pursuing an effective plan, use their powers to make things happen as they want them to happen.

Yet if we remember what the woman did, we Christians should be in a position to ask if the efficiencies of the betrayers and the plotters have the power they think. Jesus is successfully killed, yes. But his anointed body remains. This, in fact, has everything to do with the next scene in Matthew's account. After Judas the betrayer is identified (and, if we follow John, sent on his mission), something else happens. Jesus takes bread, breaks it, and gives it to his disciples, saying, take, eat, this is my body broken for you. Do this in remembrance of me. In this eating together and remembering, the disciples get connected to a power source of a quite different kind than the one the plotters and betrayers live by. As their efficiencies combine to try to crush the little band of dreamers, it is made into a new sort of community based on the memory of a broken body.

Communal Christian Life and the Memory of Judas

How this community gathers hope and new life from death and apparent defeat is the long story of the church, a story that needs to be told and remembered, although not here. For we have left Judas's story unfinished. The faithfulness of the woman who anoints Jesus is to be remembered wherever the Gospel story is told. Yet the story that is the Gospel itself, especially that of the supper, leads us back to Judas and betrayal.

In the book of Acts (1:20), we are told that the community that grew up around the memory of Jesus, the one that continues to reenact the Last Supper each week, decided to replace Judas. However, in replacing Judas the community did not forget him. In this, it did not do with Judas what Judas might have done with himself. As I have suggested, he was a lousy rememberer; he didn't have time for the woman's silly ritual of anointing Jesus with oil, and he didn't care for the leisurely chatter with Jesus and friends over dessert at the Passover supper. He wanted to get on with business.

If Judas is like Caiaphas, we might speculate about how the latter remembered the former. We are told that Judas goes to the "high priests" to arrange the deal. Let us suppose Caiaphas was involved. Do we imagine we would find in Caiaphas's record an entry "Silver, 30 pieces, to Judas Iscariot, for giving over the Galilean called Jesus"? My guess is we would not. I do suspect Caiaphas kept up a story, written—or, more likely, oral—about how he saved many people from ruin at the hands of the one blasphemous rebel Jesus. Perhaps he told it to his children in such a fashion. But I suspect Judas was not part of it. Better not to remember these messy details—especially once a successful outcome has been achieved.

Yet the Gospel story in which we read about Judas is told neither by him nor his high priest look-alike. The Gospel does not forget Judas, as Judas might have forgotten himself. Put another way, the Gospel story holds us back from getting on to business after Judas. Instead it forces us to remember him. He is there in the middle of this most important story, woven right into its central fabric. He remains in the story, and so in our memories when we retell it.

Yet the fact *that* Judas is remembered in and through the story is not the whole point. *How* he is remembered matters as well. Efficiency might have written him out; it might have forgotten Judas in order to get on with business. Yet as we have so far followed the narrative, we can see another tack, one that might put Judas to good use so as to turn the story decisively in a new direction. Another way to tell the story of Judas (that is, different from the way the Gospel tells it) would be to draw it out in terms of a dichotomy: the dualism between good and evil, light and darkness, between the unnamed faithful woman who lovingly anoints Jesus for burial and this pseudodisciple who cynically offers him the kiss of death.

There is, of course, some such contrast in the text. But the Gospel stops short of telling the story like *Star Wars*, with good on the one side, bad on the other. While John's text tells us Satan enters into Judas, neither John nor any of the other Gospel accounts demonize this man. By no means is he glorified or excused. Jesus's words are sharp-edged: "better for that one not to have been born." The truth about Judas, in other words, is that he is miserable, and his misery is infectious. But after such a terrible truth, what then? Is there a next step for Judas, or for Jesus, or for the church that remembers them both?

A contrast about how stories of miserable men work in the memory may help us focus this point. There is in American history a man who resembles Judas. This is the one who killed the excellent Alexander Hamilton (the man on the ten dollar bill) in a senseless duel. I mean the fateful Aaron Burr. Not only did he kill Hamilton, he also was tried as a traitor for some sort of complicated scheme to make money off a section of the Louisiana Purchase.

When I first learned of him in the fifth grade, Aaron Burr was unquestionably the goat of American history. Since then I have heard accounts that attempt to vindicate him somewhat. After all, he fought in the Revolutionary War, served in the Senate, and even was Thomas Jefferson's vice president. Yet American national memory of Aaron Burr is forever set by his failures. Historical scholarship might raise him up an increment or two, but he is still clearly on the other side from heroes like George Washington or Thomas Jefferson. Their legacy is triumph and success; Burr, on the other hand, remains the one who messed up.

Should we Christians remember Judas in the way Americans remember Aaron Burr? Their individual stories are similar. Yet there is an important difference, not so much in their characters but in the communities who remember them. One is a powerful and mighty nation, the other an odd group of people who claim to be the body of Christ, the very body that was broken symbolically at the Last Supper and physically the next day on the cross.

The difference between these two communities is illustrated by the difference between the Fourth of July and Easter. One we celebrate with signs of power and human invention: rockets' red glare, bombs bursting in air. The other we honor with retelling a story of suffering and death, a body broken, and by sharing a meal. American Christians sometimes forget this, imagining the national memory merely extends the church's. The symbols suggest otherwise. Fireworks on national holidays are a blast—no reason why we can't enjoy them. They light up the sky with dazzling brightness. Yet just as quickly, they fizzle and fade as the darkness overcomes them. As Christians claim, the light of the gospel shines on in the darkness, which cannot overcome it; it is a different kind of light.

What does the Gospel story do with Judas? As we early noted, when Judas slunk off to get the Roman guard, the disciples were singing a hymn and going with Jesus to the Mount of Olives. We might think that this was very high-minded and spiritual of them. But in the next verse (Matt. 26:31) we are pointed toward another conclusion. "Then Jesus said to them, 'You will all become deserters because of me this night.'" To this Peter objects: "Though all become deserters because of you, I will never desert you" (v. 33). If we know the story even a little bit, we know what happens with this heroic promise. Peter breaks it, three times in the next twenty-four hours.

In the Gospel story, Judas's sin is neither excused nor minimized. But it does not stand alone. He is joined on the sinners' bench by all the other disciples. In a way, Judas remains part of the community he chose to leave; he is remembered as one of them, one of the unfaithful twelve.

Why should we remember a story such as this? If all failed, what is the point?

The nature of the story relates to the nature of the supper these twelve shared with their master, even if one of them left before dessert. The disciples *all* took part, ate, Christ's broken body. (In Matthew, Mark, and Luke, we are not told that Judas leaves, and so we can assume he was there for the bread and wine. In John we are told that he receives a piece of bread and then immediately departs.) Because his body is broken for them, and for us, we do not have to pretend that we are whole and complete on our own.

This affects our memory especially. For whoever we are, however smooth or rocky our lives have been, we all live with memories of failure, deep disappointment, betrayal, or denial. We have known Judases. In fact we have at one time or another all acted just like him.

Christians can remember like this, telling the truth about someone we know who has left the community—perhaps someone who left a local church in anger, or a family member who turned her back on us—without either forgetting or demonizing this one. Or we can remember the truth about our own betrayals or failures. They do not need to be removed from the story, nor do they need to be demonized. In fact, they cannot be if we are to remember truthfully.

I have suggested throughout this book that this is one of the most difficult things for us to do, particularly in those communities where memory is naturally kept, family and nation. Triumph and blame are the usual companions of corporate memory. We want things to go well for us; and if they do not, we can either pretend they have, writing the whole thing down as a triumph after all, or look to find out who caused the trouble, making sure they are properly blamed and pay the penalty.

In our modern age, historians and family counselors have alerted us to the fact that peoples and families have a strong tendency to tell their stories in this way. Scientific experts in brain memory have cataloged the sort of things we tend to block or accent as we tell the story of our past to others or to ourselves. This is all very informative. But what are the alternatives? That is to say, how else might a "we" remember and tell the story of who we are and what we have come through? The experts typically offer only a sort of therapeutic neutrality, as if we might be able to rattle off a "factual" account of our past, accept it, and move on. Not only is this impossible to do, if we try, we find it empties us out, so that our story as we tell it becomes less and less ours, more and more what anyone might have gone through. The ineffectiveness of this neutralized and therapized approach is easy enough to see in our own world, where triumphalism and reverberations of blame are hardly on the decrease.

Neutrality is not the ticket. Sin and failure arise in any truthful story of the past, and they have consequences. So we must tell of them. But can we tell them of ourselves? I have suggested that stories of family and nation told in the Bible, and the tradition of Judaism that keeps the Bible alive, open us up to see where we have failed. David, for instance, with some help from Nathan the prophet, is able to see that he "is the man." Suddenly the blame he is so anxious to place on the rich man who took his poor neighbor's lone sheep turns around to point at him.

Not only does the story of the community that develops into the Christian church contain sin and failure, it has these at its root. The betrayal of Judas, the denial of Peter, and the lethargy and cowardice of the rest of the disciples is the very place where this community begins. For Paul, in fact, that is the first point of the gospel: "all have sinned and fall short of the glory of God" (Rom. 3:23)—which actually turns out to be good news, not bad, since it puts us all in the same boat and clears the room for grace. This, perhaps, is the right place for the Christian community to begin if it hopes to remember well, and in a peculiarly Christian way: to become a community of rememberers who claim no other distinction than that they are sinners who have been forgiven and reclaimed by grace.

On Not Dying Alone

We cannot deny, however, that the full truth of the Judas story is that while all the disciples sin, his sin is yet marked out as the worst. He alone is not restored to the new life of the community. Indeed, Judas comes to a horrible, lonely end. In Matthew 27 we are told that he repented of what he had done and returned the thirty pieces of silver to the authorities. After he explains himself, they reply: "What is that to us? See to it yourself." In other words, you are on your own, Judas. Then Matthew reports this: "Throwing down the pieces of silver in the temple, he departed; and he went and hanged himself" (v. 5).

As anyone who has been close to one knows, suicides are a trauma to the memory. If Judas is the betrayer, he extends the title here, for suicide seems a form of betrayal: we feel as if someone we know or love has given us the slip. Death is said to come like a thief in the night, but in suicide, it is invited in, in broad daylight. We are blinded by the sheer exposure of it, and a despair and an emptiness cuts deep into our souls. We want to cover both the exposure and the despair but know we cannot. So we do our best not to think about it, not to speak of it, not to remember it.

Usually, the memory of the death of a loved one eases with the passage of time. Early in our lives we are sometimes shocked to feel death's presence and power and may rage against so great a force. But as time carries us along, as our grandfather dies, then perhaps our grandmother, our lives change in small ways forever, but nonetheless we carry on. We come to make a certain peace with the deaths we know time will bring us, through time learning to regard them on friendlier terms.

In contrast to these deaths, suicide shocks precisely because some force other than time suddenly snatches away the one we love. For in suicide death is chosen rather than received. Suicide seems to break the rules, to strike at us from outside of the necessity of time. Try as we might, we cannot fit the suicide back into time. He dangles at the edge of our understanding, refusing to fit within the time-ful assumptions by which we live.

The Bible does nothing more to resolve for us the great shock and pain we feel in the figure of Judas. As we have mentioned, he is replaced in early Acts, so the work of the church can move onward. Perhaps it is too much to ask for some full resolution. As those who have suffered suicide know, there rarely is one. With other great sorrows of our lives, suicides cannot be put peacefully to bed in our memories, but stir there restlessly.

For Christians, the Eucharist is celebrated not only in memory but also in hope. In this way, the meal Christians share prefigures one to be had when God draws all things to completion on the last day, and the great feast of the Lamb is commenced. As Aquinas once pointed out, hope, like faith, is a "tensed" or "time-ful" virtue. Hope looks ahead to what will be but is not now. Unlike love (which remains), hope will pass away on the last day. But this accents all the more why we need it now.

Memory needs hope, else it atrophies, turning nostalgic or violent. Nostalgic memories turn away from the future and bury themselves in a falsely glorified past. The betrayals or great pains of the past are ignored; with a purposeful blindness they are removed from the memory. Violent memories have no hope, and therefore no patience; they impose their will on the world, striking out at those enemies they believe oppose their cause.

Perhaps fittingly, suicide will accommodate neither of these memory tactics. It would seem almost impossible to sentimentalize suicide—although the Hemlock Society is doing its best. Generally, though, we see the trick, especially when the suicide is close by. Similarly, we cannot use the memory of a suicide as rallying cry. We can't find the enemy—for he is the one whom we loved, now gone from us.

The Gospel story neither sentimentalizes nor vilifies Judas. His case is not finally resolved, but neither is it ignored. It is, simply, told. He remains wrapped in the story of the Last Supper, even if he leaves before it is through. As we Christians continue to celebrate this supper in hope, Judas can remain among us without becoming either monster or hero. The simple fact is perpetually placed before us: "On the night he was betrayed . . ."

In this way even Judas need not be alone in his death. We need not resolve his fate to know him as a sinner . . . as we are. It is as sinners that we come to the supper. There is, therefore, no reason why Judas cannot accompany us as we move together toward hope. As memory and hope together tell us, not one of us is fully constituted by our choices. Try as we might, we cannot choose with such force as to sever ourselves completely from all the ties that bind us to those with whom our lives are shared, and most especially with God. No one, not even Judas, is beyond hope.

According to Augustine, the eternal hope looks forward to a destination beyond this life, and this most clearly distinguishes the city of God from the earthly city. This is not to make the heavenly city unearthly. The women in the Gospel who touch and caress Jesus's body keep us from that—as does Jesus himself when he breaks the bread and commands that this very bodily thing, eating, be continued together in memory of him. What the story does, though, as it tenses this eating ("until the Lord comes"), is envision a future in which the body is made again. The memory that arises from the earth, as seed, as wheat, as bread, is pointed upward toward a "new heaven and a new earth." It is a kind of transfiguring.

If and as the church sustains and represents this new hope, it *reorients* the memory that begins with earth, with body, and with place. Neither family nor nation is based upon this hope—although there is nothing in the nature of either that must oppose it. Indeed, the problem suicide presents to the memory of family or nation may show us why certain terrors or sorrows, and perhaps certain joys, cannot be remembered well without the new hope that Christ brings.

Grief over suicide is especially strong and dangerous, for it has an overwhelming power to bring division, especially in the family. Tragic death always threatens the family, as natural or expected death does not. Family life is lived in anticipation that one generation will pass to the next. The family, in other words, is built to receive the death of the passing generation. The sadness of these deaths is easily shared within the family, since its community is a sign of the goodness of the life that has passed. This is the hope of the family: that its life will extend to subsequent generations.

Tragic death, especially of the young, cuts across this. The hope of the family does not encompass it. In suicide, the breach is deeper still, for a family member not only has been snatched away but has actually turned and departed. So the community of the family, such as it is, is separated. Not only does each one in the family of the suicide assign blame to others, or to himself or herself, they draw inward because the choice the loved one has made, the choice to leave, throws the common life of the family into question. It takes a Herculean effort for a family to hold together after a suicide.

But the church's hope is different from that of the family. As he dies, the suicide is no further from the love of God than those who die naturally, in a bed surrounded by loved ones. Neither one dies alone. God, Christians hold, is equally present with both.

This cannot mean that the two deaths are the same for us who remain. The natural death can be easily taken up into our ongoing story; the suicide cannot. It remains suspended, unresolved in any specific and common story we can tell. Yet the hope of the gospel, marked out in the Eucharist, is that the communion offered in Christ gathers in everyone. We cannot know when and how this will occur. But our hope in it allows us to carry on in the meanwhile. And so we can remember what we remember of the life and death of the loved one who committed suicide, without it tearing us apart.

This Christian hope is secured by the resurrection, whose power is most evident not in a resuscitated corpse, but by a regathered community, the church, whose common life and shared weekly meal points ahead to the kingdom yet to come. In the narrative of the Gospels, the resurrection comes after not only Judas's betrayal but also his suicide. It encompasses both, reminding those of us who live in the hope of the resurrection that death cannot be the final word. While Judas's betrayal and suicide have great power on earth, in family and community life, the resurrection speaks a greater word that is carried forward by the church in its patented hope. The destructive power the betrayer and the suicide have brought into the world is great, but not so great as to separate him forever from the love of God, who patiently yet tirelessly seeks to gather all things unto himself.

9

Re-membering by Baptism

Minding the Gap between Memory and Hope

According to reports, potentially groundbreaking scientific research is currently being undertaken to unlock the secret of memory. An edition of a major news magazine I picked up tied these developments to a slimy little spotted sea snail named *Aplysia californicus*, which will help us probe memory's depths. How splendid!

Likely we should be doing scientific research of this sort, even if with slightly less pomp. However, it is difficult not to feel something of an incongruity within the idea of "memory research," particularly because we are all thoroughly aware of just how strange our memory can be. Each of us has little nodules of vividness floating about in our brains, precise bits of recall that, out of nowhere, can suddenly leap into the forefront of our memory and display a scene from our past as if it occurred last hour, when its actual date might be thirty years prior. The question we ask in such circumstances is always: why do I remember that—especially when I have not the slightest idea where I last put down the car keys? Concerning the upcoming major scientific breakthroughs, we are led to wonder: when the fantastic new drug of pureed *Aplysia* is ready and we drink it down, will these tiny memory nodules suddenly overtake our minds? This is the stuff of a sci-fi thriller. But the premise is not so silly. In our quest to remember so well, will our minds become so full of vivid little nodules of memory that we will forget what we need to remember the most?

Were they not so close to unlocking the secret of memory, I should like to ask some scientist if there is a pattern to these vivid flashes of memory, these little moments in my brain that I seem so unable to forget. Speaking entirely unscientifically, while some of these vivid moments seem to have nothing much to do with anything, a disproportionate number seem associated with a disturbance of some kind in family or national life. People often speak of remembering exactly where they were when they heard that President John F. Kennedy had been shot. I was in the third grade, and I remember hearing it. We got off school early, and I remember that—particularly going home on the bus wondering what it all meant. Or, more recently, I remember exactly where I was, what street I was turning onto in my car in my daily commute to work, when I first heard the NPR report, interjected into the middle of a regular newscast on the morning of September 11, 2001, that a plane had reportedly just crashed into one of the towers of the World Trade Center. I suspect it is the same for most Americans. The details of that day stand out in sharp relief.

Perhaps the scientists could tell me that this vividness in memory comes from a spike in endorphins or brain chemicals of this or that sort. This would be interesting news. But I should like to know how this works *humanly*. Again completely unscientifically, I will venture a guess. The vivid sequences of recollection each of us has stored in our brains are weighted heavily toward circumstances in which news is anxiously received. Something comes to us that threatens or upsets life as we know it, and we are for a while suspended in time. Oh, oh, oh! And we think: now what—now what?

In these moments a wide gap seems suddenly to open up between memory and hope. As we have discussed, these two are intertwined. How we hope affects how we remember, and vice versa. Without noticing it, we live daily into a hope; we envision a future that carries our past forward in a certain way. As we live toward hope, memory accompanies us, gathering our past up in such a way as to point it toward our hope, whatever it may be. (As noted, if Christians' final hope is in the resurrection, this cannot but change the direction of their memory.)

As we are carried along in a nation by memory, now and then we suddenly find ourselves lost in these gaps between hope and memory. An event comes that we know instinctively is of great national significance, and for the moment we feel as if we have lost hold of the future. Later, that moment returns vividly to us. It seems burned into our memory forever.

Hope That Lives by Love and Faith

Often the national events we remember receiving news of are horrible ones, like September 11, 2001. Horror likely enhances the vividness by which we remember, but not solely horror. For instance, many of us remember vividly the news of Richard Nixon's resignation as president. As for me, I was just old enough to have formed the political opinion that this was a very good thing, given the circumstances. But the occasion of hearing the news (and seeing Nixon's announcement on television) remains with me vividly.

A similar dynamic fits many of the events in family life we remember with this kind of vividness. We receive news that is sure to change how we will go on. The news is frequently bad, but not always. For instance, I recall with vividness getting the news from my wife that she was pregnant with our first child. More than that of birth, news brought of the death of someone in the family whom we love seems especially prominent on the list of things we can never forget. I can remember with precision the phone call that came from my sister to say that our father had suffered a heart attack on the tarmac at the Toronto airport. I was eating breakfast on the porch when the phone rang, and I stood in the doorway between the porch and the kitchen while we went over the details.

We have already discussed a case of this: King David waiting over the city gate for news of the death of his son Absalom. Nicholas Wolterstorff poignantly tells of another at the beginning of his remarkable book *Lament for a Son*. We can tell as we read it that the details Wolterstorff reports are burned forever into his memory.

> The call came at 3:30 on that Sunday afternoon, a bright sunny day. We had just sent a younger brother off to the plane to be with him for the summer.
> "Mr. Wolterstorff?"—"Yes."—"Is this Eric's father?"—"Yes."—"Mr. Wolterstorff, I must give you some bad news."—"Yes."—"Eric has been climbing in the mountains and he had an accident."—"Yes."—"Eric has had a serious accident."—"Yes."—"Mr. Wolterstorff, I must tell you, Eric is dead. Mr. Wolterstorff, are you there? You must come at once! Mr. Wolterstorff, Eric is dead."
> For three seconds I felt the peace of resignation: arms extended, limp son in hand, peacefully offering him to someone—Someone. Then the pain—cold burning pain. (9)

As Wolterstorff proceeds through his many "yeses," we can feel his anxiety grow. What is coming? Where is my Eric? What will we do? His attention is not fixed on the change—he is thinking about Eric—but he nonetheless knows that news delivered on the phone will mark a sharp turn in the story of his family. The moment we are taken through in this paragraph will soon become the point in the Wolterstorffs' lives that marks the before and after: before and after Eric's death.

It is by story that we move through time, with a past, a present, a future. Memory and hope set this pattern as we proceed from what was to what will be. The kind of story we are in has everything to do with their interaction. Between memory and hope stands something more. It is love. By hope we press on to a destination that lies above and beyond us. By memory we know how to mark progress, how to connect one bit of our past to other bits so as to gather up where and what we have been into a meaningful pattern that we can build upon. Yet neither hope nor memory makes any sense without love. By love our lives come to be knit with others such that it makes sense to call some memories precious. And by love hope becomes shared, making the story of any one of us more than merely our own.

In moments such as the one Wolterstorff remembers so vividly, love and hope seem to oppose one another. Hopes build naturally within us as we live out our earthly lives, from the ground up. We come to assume a direction for our lives; we assume we will grow and flourish and that those we love will grow with us. Yet events come upon us—we receive news—that takes what we love from us, and so throws into disarray a past that has been building up as hope. We have learned to love by hope, but our love, now lost, dismantles hope. The story turns back upon itself; our memories seem to scatter, or become bitter to us, seeming like cruel and false promises.

Wolterstorff writes out the story of the death of his son as a Christian. His book, which proceeds onward *after* Eric's death, is the story of a faith that grounds and reconnects hope and love. As we look to see how this works, we can learn something of the significance of the Christian triad of theological virtues: faith, hope, and love. Of these, faith is almost always listed first. Love comes last because it, say both Paul and Aquinas, is the greatest of these. Yet faith is necessary as a first term for the other two to grow up properly.

Of the three virtues, faith is the least natural. Hope and love, some form of them, grow up from the ground. Both grasp for something we need and want, and there is nothing more "natural" than this. As such, hope and love can clutch and hold on tight. Faith is what opens our clutching hands and offers what we have to God. By faith, says Paul, Abraham could offer up Isaac his son. Similarly, it is Nicholas Wolterstorff's faith that allows him to feel, if only for three seconds, "the peace of resignation: arms extended, limp son in hand, peacefully offering him to someone—Someone." Faith is all about letting go of what we naturally (and rightly) love and hope for; as such, faith opens our hopes and loves to the perfecting power of God's love. Reoriented by faith, hope and love can open us out to a new future that extends beyond the earthly life to the heavenly.

Thomas Aquinas has much to say on these matters, so much that it is easy to get lost. Yet as is almost always the case with Aquinas, an accessible insight lies beneath his detailed schema. Faith, Aquinas says, is associated with our intellect; it is related to knowledge, and its object is truth (see II–II, 1–9). As related to knowledge it has a special quality: as the author of Hebrews says, it is "conviction of things not seen" (11:1)—which is why faith is not science (II–II, 1, 2).

The association with the intellect and the direct tie to truth distinguishes faith from hope and love, which are rooted rather in the "appetites" or "passions." In the final analysis we must not only have faith in God, but also love him forever, which is why love exceeds both faith and hope as "the greatest" of all (1 Cor. 13:13). But faith opens the door, the one Christ knocks on. And, as I believe, it does so with memory.

Memories rise up in our minds like little sprouts from the ground. There is nothing abstract about them at all. They are about body and place, and so they tie us to land and blood. Left to grow on their own, they can become strong and intertwine into a matrix of connected branches that supports individual and communal life. Yet nothing about this growth guarantees that the forest of memory will not become so thick as to block out the truth. In fact, we all know that impassioned hopes and loves, especially those that have been with us for some time, can keep us from the light of truth.

The intellectual calmness of faith opens us to a world different from that dominated by our natural hopes and loves. In fact, it ties us to the truth that "our world" comes not from us but from God. "By faith we understand that the worlds were prepared by the word of God, so that what is seen was made from things that are not visible" (Heb. 11:3). And so faith offers us another sort of thing to do with our memories than what those memories themselves might be urging upon us.

Passion associated with natural loves and hopes springs forth with great force when either is threatened or thwarted. So we strike out, or cover up, or plot, all to keep our love or hope alive. The alternative path—opened by faith, and which Wolterstorff takes—is simply to offer them up. Doing so does not reduce the pain of loves and hopes lost and broken, which Wolterstorff feels as "cold and burning." But it positions that pain in relation to the truth Christians know by faith, namely, that the God of the universe sustains all our lives in perfect love and, in the end, gathers them unto himself.

An Unmemorable Baptism

It may be a sign of my own impiety, but I do not remember "Christian" events very well. The other day it became necessary to determine just what was the date of our daughter's baptism. I had not the slightest idea, nor, for that matter, did my wife. A frantic search yielded the certificate in a file somewhere, and we were much relieved.

I was raised in a little Christian denomination, the Plymouth Brethren, who are akin to Garrison Keillor's first Christian group. We made a great deal of "getting saved." You worry in your early years about its not having happened yet, if and when it does you feel great relief, and from then on you have to work your best to keep the details clear and vivid in your memory. The clear and vivid remembrance works as a sort of stamp of validity. Unfortunately for me, the details fairly quickly faded in my mind. Later on as a teenager, it came time to tell the story to the group of leading brethren who came to talk with me to see whether I was fit for full church membership. While I don't recall exactly what I said about how I got saved, I do remember that it was exaggerated.

It seems to me to be an ill-advised strategy for Christians to try to compete head to head with family, or even nation, in the category of vivid remembrance. That is, if the church, like the family and the nation, is a sort of community of memory (and I believe it is), and it needs on certain matters to challenge the memories that run along in family or nation (which I believe it sometimes does), it should not try to do so on the basis of the vividness or power of certain sets of memories of churchy or Christian events.

I do not mean to say the church should not try to have a memorable common life or that it is not significant that we sometimes look back with great comfort and joy to this or that special occasion in church, such as festive gatherings at Easter or Christmas time. If we listen to Moses, we should know that how we mark our calendar matters, and if we do this according to the narrative of the life of Israel or of Jesus, we will remember better as a people.

But the deepest power of Christian memory does not lie in the excitement or the memorability of the events that it sponsors. For Christian memory is not principally concerned with what we feel as we remember, or even how vividly the memories come to us, but rather with where our memory leads us in thought, word, and deed. The church is less a *producer* of memories than it is a *trainer* of those memories that arise elsewhere, family and nation being the two prominent places in which production is wrought.

The church's main function is not to produce memorable events for its people. We can see more about how this works when we notice that, while the church should try to make events memorable (for instance, to try to avoid making sermons boring and unmemorable), it sometimes must consciously decide to make them less memorable than they could be. My daughter's baptism was such an event. Here's what I remember: Our pastor Henry was an older man whom we liked and respected a good deal. We assumed it was he who would baptize our little girl. However, when we gathered a few days before the event to cover the details, Henry said that he very much hoped that another pastor, his new assistant, John, would do the actual baptizing. John had been ordained just a few months before and had not yet had a chance to preside directly at a baptism.

Now, while John was a fine man and we had no quarrels with him, he was not Henry. And we had envisioned Henry's hands holding Claire while the water washed over her head. We had anticipated her snuggled in Henry's arms as he walked about in the aisles of the congregation showing her to all present while we all sang a song of welcome—a moving local baptismal practice Henry himself had instituted. Both my wife and I left the prebaptism meeting a little chagrined. But we went along with the plan, John baptized Claire, and we are all none the worse off for it. In fact, we might be better off. For while we may not remember the occasion of our daughter's baptism with the thrill we might had Henry officiated, we have learned something about why this sort of memory is not the kind that carries the day.

In 1 Corinthians, Paul chides members of the church in Corinth for rivalries that had arisen, in part, over who was baptized by whom. He expresses relief that he baptized only a couple of the Corinthians, "so that no one can say you were baptized in my name" (1 Cor. 1:15). He then goes on to say:

> And so, brothers and sisters, I could not speak to you as spiritual people, but rather as people of the flesh, as infants in Christ. I fed you with milk, not solid food, for you were not ready for solid food. Even now you are still not ready, for you are still of the flesh. For as long as there is jealousy and quarreling among you, are you not of the flesh, and behaving according to human inclinations? For when one says, "I belong to Paul," and another, "I belong to Apollos," are you not merely human?
> What then is Apollos? What is Paul? Servants through whom you came to believe, as the Lord assigned to each. I planted, Apollos watered, but God gave the growth. (1 Cor. 3:1–6)

A key part of the church's job is to remind us that we don't matter half as much as we think we do. This includes our memories. We do not go to church to accumulate a collection of so many memorable events. Despite claims to the contrary in some of America's contemporary churches, when we assemble for worship, the point is not to have the best worship experience you've ever had—one that you'll never forget. For the church, especially the church at worship, is not really about us, but about Christ, who, Paul says in the next verses, is its sole foundation.

Family life *is* about us, about our growth and decline, about the birth of our children and the death of our parents and grandparents. We are rightly carried along by the story of the family, which hands us different roles to play out over the full course of our lives. There is a time to be born and a time to die, a time to plant and a time to uproot, a time to seek and a time to cast away. Like the earth to which it related, family life is guided by seasons. We rightly celebrate their turnings, and these celebrations and turnings will attach themselves to our memories in ways that other events rarely will: the birth of a child, a honeymoon, the death of a parent.

Similarly, a nation's life is about those of us who live in it. Huge, memorable events come to nations as they are attacked by other nations or suffer natural calamities of various sorts. As with families, their future is never secure, and they can take marked turns in their development. When they do, we notice and later remember, since the story carried by the nation is about us and how we are faring. Dramatic turns of events burn a path into our brain, and we store it there, indefinitely.

Unlike family and nation, the church does not begin and end with us. Its first job, as just noted, is to remind us that the story of the universe does not have us at its center. As the church tells us on Ash Wednesday: "Remember that you are dust, and to dust you shall return." Beyond this, it points us to Christ, who is the head of the church. The object of church life is to learn to point our lives in his direction.

This is not to say that this trajectory in church life should be designed to leave us out. We are, after all, the body of Christ. When we partake in his body broken and eaten as bread, we partake, as Augustine notes, of ourselves. Yet as Paul would have it, the "us" here is not fleshly, but spiritual people. Membership in Christ's body makes us new, and a sign of this will be that we do not feel compelled to use the events of our lives as Christians to subsidize our own family or national stories. Baptism, for instance, can be an event in which a family participates with great joy, but it is first and foremost an event in the church. Never should we design baptism so that it serves the life and story of the family, as if our chief concern is that they remember it fondly and well. Instead, baptism calls the baptized, and his or her families, to see that the life they have together as a family must point not back to itself but beyond to Christ, whose body they are joining.

Renewing the Baptismal Covenant

The service of baptism in the Anglican *Book of Common Prayer* begins with some questions to the candidates and/or their parents and godparents. With their answers they renounce Satan and claim Christ. Then the congregation assembled gets a chance to chime in about whether they will support the newly baptized in their life in Christ. After this the celebrant says: "Let us join with those who are committing themselves to Christ and renew our own baptismal covenant."

This is interesting. The invitation is for those assembled to look back over their own lives in a certain way. How are they to do this? Are they to think back to the feel of the water splashing over their heads or the feel of the oil as it is pressed, warm and wet, onto their forehead? While it would not necessarily be wrong to do this, if this is our concentration we have missed the point. (The fact that many of us were baptized as children may help here. There is simply no experience hidden in our memories to call up, so we are not tempted to make more of it than we ought.)

Baptism is the most significant event in the life of an individual Christian, since it is the means by which she or he enters God's life in the church. As such, we must remember it. But we need to get right what the "remembering" means. Once again, it is not so important that we be transported in memory back to the occasion of our baptism—which, in our different memories, some can do vividly, others vaguely, and many not at all. When the church tells us to remember our baptism, it is not getting at this kind of memory. Rather it is urging us to *renew* in our present lives what occurred at baptism, namely, that we became children of God's kingdom. As such, the church means to train our memory *spiritually*.

Baptism is about the flesh, yes, for we need the touch of the actual water administered by the actual hand of one who represents the visible church. But it is also about the spirit. This is how Paul is using the term *spiritual* when he scolds the Corinthians for being too "fleshly" in their thinking about baptism when they want Paul and not Apollos, or Henry and not John, to do the honors. The mistake is like the one Nicodemus makes when he thinks about being "born again" as a reentrance into his mother's womb (John 3:4). Jesus answers there, "Very truly, I tell you, no one can enter the kingdom of God without being born of water and Spirit. What is born of the flesh is flesh, and what is born of the Spirit is spirit. Do not be astonished that I said to you, 'You must be born from above'" (3:5–7).

In baptism, the bodily life of family and nation meets the spiritual life of the church. The spiritual life of the church does not destroy the life of the body; rather, it gathers it up into a new spiritual body: Christ's. We must not mistake the "spiritual body" as ethereal. We are still speaking about real human bodies, as Paul's next complaint to the Corinthians makes clear. He tells them that precisely because they are members of Christ's body they should not be joining that body sexually with prostitutes (1 Cor. 6:16–17).

Perhaps the best way to put the point is that membership in the body of Christ (or baptism "by water and the spirit," or being "born from above"—however you like it) "spiritually" reorients bodily life, opening some ways of being bodies in the world and closing off others. Both the "remembering me [Christ]" that Christians do at Eucharist and the renewing of their baptismal covenant spiritually reorient bodily memory.

Bodily memory is the sort we have been discussing for most of this book. It is the memory that rises up from the ground, the memory carried by family and nation. The imagery here, as before with Romero on the mount of transfiguration, is vertical. By family and nation we are born from below into the life of the body; by water and spirit we are raised with Christ to new life. The new life of memory, though, does not replace bodily memory. It does not even compete with it for the highest degree of vividness. Instead, it continually reminds bodily memory where it cannot turn: not to violence, or bitterness, or despair, or worry, or vengeance, or vilification, or scapegoating, or falsity, or even to spin.

The clearest way to understand the spiritual transformation worked in baptism is to recall that by it we enter a covenant. This is the covenant the *Book of Common Prayer* asks everyone to renew as they participate as church in the baptism of a new one. The words of this renewal begin with a personalized version of the Apostles' Creed, in question form: "Do you believe in God the Father?—I believe in God, the Father Almighty . . ."

The covenant, in other words, begins as an affirmation of *faith*. Faith opens a door to a new life. But now the life needs to take a specific shape. Faith leads to offerings, to promises, and to action. So, after personally affirming the creed, we are pressed on to continue in the apostles' teaching and the breaking of bread, to resist evil and to repent of our sins, to proclaim by word and example the good news of God in Christ, and to serve Christ in all persons, loving our neighbors as ourselves, striving for justice and peace among all people, and respecting the dignity of every human being.

As circumcision did for Jews or Odysseus's scar did for him, baptism actually is supposed to contain us, keeping us from being whoever we want to be, reminding us that wherever we wander Christ will come along. But it does more than this. The mark or "seal" we bear through baptism makes us members of the family of God and citizens in Christ's kingdom. So beyond containing us within and in relation to a past, baptism also seals us and directs us toward a future when we will be remade by the God of the universe into more than we have been so far. Left alone, the memory of family and nation points back to itself. Christian memory, by contrast, has a destination beyond itself. Looking back to our baptism, remembering that we are among the baptized who have been joined in Christ's body, becomes a springboard into the future. The life opened up to us when we are claimed as Christ's own is life in the coming kingdom, a life that has even now already arrived.

Adopting and Re-membering

Some family friends, Demery and Scott, had been considering adoption since they were first married. Then came September 11, 2001. They could wait no longer; they had to act now. As Demery put it, as a family they simply felt they needed to offer an answer to this horrible event. They could do nothing to bring back those who died, or to comfort the mourners, but they could gather up a small, precious life that needed a home. So they went down to the offices in Scranton, filed the papers, and began the bureaucratic rigmarole all adoptive parents come to know much better than they would like to.

About three months after this first filing in October of 2001, we got a call from Demery, who sounded a bit rattled. The agency had called; they had a little newborn baby boy who needed to be taken home from the hospital that day. Any thoughts? Would we pray for them?

Eli came to join Scott, Demery, and Nolan in the summer following 9/11. He was at that time officially a ward of the state, and so to them officially a foster child. But they immediately claimed him fully as their own. This actually created a dilemma. For if he was theirs, they would want him baptized. Membership in their family opened immediately upward to membership in Christ's body. The dilemma arose in that, so long as Eli was a foster child, his participation in religious rites required consent of the birth mother. Scott and Demery received permission to bring Eli to church, but they wisely refrained from asking how far permission to "bring him to church" extended (when in a bureaucracy, do as the bureaucrats do). Despite their expressed concern to the state's representatives that Eli become their adoptive child as soon as this could be arranged, there was one holdup after another at the bureaucratic level, and the months dragged on and on. Finally, they decided (with my wife's and my complicity, since we were to be Eli's godparents) that Eli should be claimed as Christ's own forever.

The baptism proceeded like any other; Eli was washed and sealed and entered the church. His biological story will differ in certain respects from the rest of his family's, but his familial story will not. He has been fully grafted into both family and church community. If he does not learn it from his baptism, he will learn from his family that membership in Christ's body means that it is possible for communities to open out, to welcome strangers as full members, and go on with joy and hope—a rather stark contrast to the lesson taken in some circles from the crisis of 9/11.

Eli's case illustrates the many points of both potential cooperation and potential tension that can arise between the three communities we have been discussing: family, church, and nation. But further, it brings into focus important language in the New Testament about what the church is up to as it gathers in members from among the families and nations of the world. Particularly because Gentile Christians saw themselves as having been received into a family for which they lacked biological pedigree, the family of Abraham, *adoption* was the first language of description for how the church grew. For instance, in Ephesians we hear: "He destined us for adoption as his children through Jesus Christ, according to the good pleasure of his will" (1:5).

In contrast to biological parenting, we sometimes imagine that adoption is about choice rather than about receiving what is given—as if adoptive parents might say to their new children, "You're special because we liked your little dimply cheeks the best." Yet here in Ephesians, and elsewhere in Paul's letters, adoption into the family of God is not about choice based on special characteristics. Adoption is destiny. Our call into God's family is a given, even a gift. Not through any special merits of our own, we are meant to be in it. This assists rather than resists memory. For memory, as we have said, is mainly about what we have been given rather than what we choose.

But perhaps more importantly, what the story of the adoption of the Gentiles tells us is that the church is a unity of all peoples everywhere. According to the author of Ephesians, this sets the tenor of the community and the attitudes and action of those within it. "I . . . beg you to lead a life worthy of the calling to which you have been called, with all humility and gentleness, with patience, bearing with one another in love, making every effort to maintain the unity of the Spirit in the bond of peace. There is one body and one Spirit, just as you were called to the one hope of your calling, one Lord, one faith, one baptism, one God and Father of all" (Eph. 4:1–6).

Augustine expands on this point as he sketches out the whole story of the City of God on earth. In fact, by origin there is only one human family—we are all of the same stock from Adam and Eve. The City of God marks this unity not only as it looks back to this origin but as it looks ahead to the one final destination we share, namely, the heavenly peace, "the perfectly ordered and harmonious communion of those who find their joy in God and one another in God" (*City of God*, 19.17).

It may sound too clever to be true, but the church's work is to *re-member* as it remembers. The words "remembering" or "recollecting" suggest a gathering together of what otherwise is scattered. Christian baptism, especially understood as adoption, carries this same imagery. We are gathered in from all human families to the new family of God. But the new is also the old, since we were in the first place created for fellowship with God. The breakup of the first family, Adam and Eve's rebellion, Cain's fratricide, Babel's pride, have scattered us into many families and nations whose stories are about their own past and no other. As the first fruits of the kingdom of God, the church regathers what has become scattered and separate; humankind is re-membered with itself and with God.

In the regathering, the trick is to re-member without merging. The kingdom of God is not like a great melting pot. In Augustine's language, "So long, then, as the heavenly City is wayfaring on earth, she invites citizens from all nations and all tongues, and unites them into a single pilgrim band. She takes no issue with that diversity of customs, laws and traditions whereby human peace is sought and maintained. Instead of nullifying or tearing down, she preserves and appropriates whatever in the diversities of divers races is aimed at one and the same object of human peace"(19.17). Or, as we have been saying, the memory that is carried along by the church does not displace or supersede that of the families and nations it calls up into itself. Peculiarities and diversities of memories and cultures arise from the great variety of places each of us calls home. We dig ourselves into the soil and grow, over time accumulating memories of family and nation that are unlike any other. Gathered together under the peace of the eternal city, these diverse memories can thrive and be shared.

Of course this is not the shape of our current world. Separate histories have bred separate and warring identities. Greed for land, the desire for ascendancy of one set of memories or stories over all the others, the perverse will to be left alone so as to oppress or rape or enslave one's own people—these are the very real elements that haunt the memories of nations and families. Even today such elements strengthen and grow under many false names. It is no wonder some choose, like Odysseus, to break free from it all and wander alone on the surging sea.

But there is, in the end, no escaping. We are children of our parents, born in lands that have been raked over a thousand times by men and women who went before us and who built, for better or worse, the political entities to which we are linked by patrimony. Those of us who are Christians, along with certain others who travel under different names, think we have glimpsed a way whereby we can remain in the midst of the communities that form us but also look beyond to a wider future in the land of peace. There is nothing more important for us to do than remember well in our families and nations and to continue the long work of re-membering God's family (or God's kingdom; it is the same under either name) in hope of the final day of harvest, when the wheat will be gathered in and separated from the tares, justice shall ascend the throne, and we shall all gather together at the feet of the Lamb that was slain.

Works Cited

Aquinas, St. Thomas. *Summa Theologica*. Translated by the English Dominican Province. New York: Benziger Brothers, 1948.

Augustine. *City of God*. Translated by Gerald G. Walsh, et. al. New York: Doubleday, 1958.

———. *Confessions*. Translated by F. J. Sheed. Indianapolis: Hackett, 1993.

Barth, Karl. *Church Dogmatics* III/4. Translated by A. T. Mackay, et al. Edinburgh: T & T Clark, 1961.

Bellah, Robert, Richard Madsen, William M. Sullivan, et al. *Habits of the Heart: Individualism and Commitment in American Life*. Berkeley: University of California Press, 1985.

Berry, Wendell. *The Hidden Wound*. New York: North Point, 1989.

Bonhoeffer, Dietrich. *Ethics*. Translated by Neville Horton Smith. New York: Macmillan, 1963.

Book of Common Prayer (1979). New York: Oxford University Press, 2000.

Brockman, James R. *Romero: A Life*. Maryknoll, NY: Orbis, 1990.

Fretheim, Terence E. *Exodus*. Louisville: Westminster John Knox Press, 1991.

Geach, Peter. *God and the Soul*. Chicago: St. Augustine's, 2001.

Hauerwas, Stanley. *Against the Nations: War and Survival in a Liberal Society*. New York: Winston, 1985.

———. *The Peaceable Kingdom: A Primer in Christian Ethics*. Notre Dame, IN: University of Notre Dame Press, 1983.

Homer. *The Iliad*. Translated by Robert Fitzgerald. New York: Anchor, 1974.

———. *The Odyssey*. Translated by Robert Fitzgerald. New York: Vintage, 1990.

John Paul II. *Memory and Identity*. New York: Rizzoli, 2005.

Kass, Leon R. *Toward a More Natural Science*. New York: Free Press, 1985.

———, and Amy A. Kass, eds. *Wing to Wing, Oar to Oar: Readings on Courting and Marrying*. Notre Dame, IN: University of Notre Dame Press, 2001.

Lasch, Christopher. *Haven in a Heartless World: The Family Besieged*. New York: W. W. Norton, 1995.

Locke, John. *An Essay concerning Human Understanding*. Buffalo: Prometheus, 1994.

Lott, Bret. *A Song I Knew by Heart*. New York: Random House, 2004.

Neuhaus, Richard. *The Naked Public Square*. Grand Rapids: Eerdmans, 1986.

O'Donovan, Oliver. *The Desire of the Nations: Rediscovering the Roots of Political Theology*. New York: Cambridge University Press, 1996.

Platt, Barbara L. *This Is Holy Ground: A History of the Gettysburg Battlefield*. Harrisburg, PA: Huggins Printing, 2001.

Porter, Joan. *Nature as Reason: A Thomistic Theory of Natural Law*. Grand Rapids: Eerdmans, 2004.

Ricoeur, Paul. Translated by Kathleen Blamey and David Pellauer. *Memory, History, Forgetting*. Chicago: University of Chicago Press, 2004.

Romero, Oscar. *Voice of the Voiceless: The Four Pastoral Letters and Other Statements*. Translated by Michael J. Walsh. Maryknoll, NY: Orbis, 1990.

Shaara, Michael. *The Killer Angels*. New York: Ballantine, 1987.

Sobrino, Jon. *Witnesses to the Kingdom: The Martyrs of El Salvador and the Crucified Peoples*. Maryknoll, NY: Orbis, 2003.

Tyler, Anne. *Saint Maybe*. New York: Ivy Books, 1992.

Wells, Samuel, and Stanley Hauerwas, eds. *The Blackwell Companion to Christian Ethics*. New York: Blackwell, 2004.

Wolterstorff, Nicholas. *Lament for a Son*. Grand Rapids: Eerdmans, 1987.